Trading Stocks
By the Numbers

Trading Stocks By the Numbers

FINANCIAL ENGINEERING FOR PROFIT

Grant Henning PhD

Copyright © 2015 Grant Henning PhD
All rights reserved.

ISBN: 1517283264
ISBN 13: 9781517283261
Library of Congress Control Number: 2015915039
CreateSpace Independent Publishing Platform
North Charleston, South Carolina

Dedication

This work is dedicated first to the memory of my parents who, though not having a college education themselves, taught me to persevere in study to solve life's problems.

It is also dedicated to my dear wife, Ruth, who has been with me through most of this exciting journey of life as an example of resourcefulness, hospitality, perseverance, and courage.

It is also dedicated to my two children and seven grandchildren—especially my son, Jeffrey, who is the best trader I know and who has been my constant sounding board.

Finally, it is dedicated to Professor Charles Cao, Chairman of the Finance Department at Smeal College of Business, the Pennsylvania State University, for his friendship and encouragement and his exemplary teaching and research.

Table of Contents

	Preface · xi
Introduction	A Background Rationale for the Use of Mathematical Models in Stock Trading · · · · · · · · · · · · xv
Chapter 1	Defining a Portfolio Database · 1
	Summary: · 6
PART ONE	TECHNICALS · 9
Chapter 2	Percentage Lag (Proximity to New Highs) · · · · · · · · · 11
	Evaluation and Summary: · · · · · · · · · · · · · · · · · · · 13
Chapter 3	Momentum · 15
	Summary: · 19
Chapter 4	Price-Action Ranking · 20
	Summary: · 23
Chapter 5	Regression Residuals · 24
	Summary: · 31
Chapter 6	The Relative Strength Index (RSI) and The Cumulative Technical Ranking Index (CTR) · · · · · · · · 32
	Summary of Part One · 35
PART TWO	FUNDAMENTALS · 39
Chapter 7	Choosing Fundamental Indices · · · · · · · · · · · · · · · · · 41
	Price-to-Sales Ratio (PSR) · · · · · · · · · · · · · · · · · · · 46
	Earnings per Share (EPS) · · · · · · · · · · · · · · · · · · · 48
	Five-Year Annual Sales Growth (5YSG) · · · · · · · · · 49

        Return on Assets (ROA) · · · · · · · · · · · · · · · · · · 49
        Profit Margin (PM) · 50
        Combining Ranks · 50
        Summary · 52

PART THREE COMPOSITE RANKINGS OF STOCKS · · · · · · · · · · · · · · 53
Chapter 8   Global Aggregate Ranks · 55
        Deriving a Global Total Ranking Index · · · · · · · · 55
        The Technical-Fundamental Discrepancy Index · · 58
        Aggregation for Decision Making · · · · · · · · · · · · 59
        Deriving a Universal Index · · · · · · · · · · · · · · · · 60
        Summary: · 66

PART FOUR **TRADING STRATEGIES** · 67
Chapter 9   Implementing Momentum Trading Strategies · · · · · · · 69
        1.   The Percentage Lag Strategy · · · · · · · · · · · · · 70
        2.   The One-Month Momentum Strategy · · · · · · 71
        3.   The Cumulative Momentum Strategy · · · · · · · 73
        4.   The Multiple Ratio Momentum Strategy · · · · · 74
        5.   The Patterned Price Movement Strategy · · · · · 75
        Summary: · 75
Chapter 10 Implementing Performance Trading Strategies · · · · · · 77
        1.   The One-Month Gain Strategy · · · · · · · · · · · · · 77
        2.   The Universal Index Strategy · · · · · · · · · · · · · 78
        3.   The Global Total Performance Strategy · · · · · 79
        4.   The Comprehensive Performance Strategy · · · 80
        5.   The Future Trend Strategy · · · · · · · · · · · · · · · 81
        Strategies Compared · 82
        Summary: · 85

PART FIVE **MARKET TIMING AND LEVERAGING** · · · · · · · · · · · 87
Chapter 11 Timing Indicators · 89
        Macro Timing Indicators · · · · · · · · · · · · · · · · · · · 90
           PE Averages and RSI Averages · · · · · · · · · · · 90
           VIX Trends and Put/Call Ratios · · · · · · · · · · · 91

	Micro Timing Indicators · · · · · · · · · · · · · · · · · · · 92	
	1. The Relative Strength Index (RSI) Trend Line · 94	
	2. The Volume Indicator Histogram · · · · · · · 95	
	3. The Moving Average Convergence/ Divergence (MACD) Histogram and Moving Average Crossovers · · · · · · · · · · · 95	
	4. The ADX Trend Lines · · · · · · · · · · · · · · · · 97	
	Timing Indicators Compared · · · · · · · · · · · · · · · · 97	
	Summary: · 99	
Chapter 12	Leverage · 100	
	Risk · 100	
	Using Margin · 101	
	Leveraged Bull and Bear Funds · · · · · · · · · · · · · · 103	
	Options · 103	
	Summary · 104	
Chapter 13	Afterthoughts and Wrapping Up · · · · · · · · · · · · · 105	
	Housekeeping Issues · 106	
	1. What should be done about missing data? · 106	
	2. How often should data be updated? · · · · 106	
	3. What may be the most suitable criteria for adding and deleting stocks from the database? · · · · · · · · · · · · · · · · · 107	
	4. How dependable are internet data sources? · 108	
	Recent Insights · 108	
	Interval Gains Ranking · · · · · · · · · · · · · · · · · 108	
	New Prediction Variables · · · · · · · · · · · · · · · 109	
	Research Needed · 112	
	Perspective · 115	
Index A	List of Tables · 117	
Index B	List of Figures · 119	
Index C	Recommended Websites · · · · · · · · · · · · · · · · · · · 121	
Index D	Recommended Readings · · · · · · · · · · · · · · · · · · · 123	

Preface

This is intended as a sequel to my earlier book published in 2010 by Wiley & Sons under the title *The Value and Momentum Trader: Dynamic Stock Selection Models to Beat the Market.* That book captured my continuing philosophy of and approach to trading and was accompanied by an Excel DVD with an actual preliminary spreadsheet that allowed any trader to input data from current stocks of interest and obtain a mathematical ranking of stocks at any given time to aid decisions of buying and selling. The book was reasonably well received in worldwide distribution and is still available online or possibly also at your local library.

This present work is not designed to replace that book, but only to complement it by adding additional new information. Therefore, the reader is encouraged to begin with that work to obtain necessary basic information that will not be revisited here. The essential vocabulary and syntax of trading will not be defined or explained in this book, but the assumption is made that the reader is already informed about necessary terminology and practice—what I there termed the vocabulary and syntax of trading. In the previous book an extensive introductory bibliography was presented so that the novice could quickly gather auxiliary information to grasp the fundamental features of trading. Unlike that prior publication, the present book is not accompanied by any preprogrammed Excel DVD, so there is an assumption here that the reader will already have obtained or gained access to such software in order to implement mathematical trading systems. What is unique in this book is a systematic presentation of lessons learned in the intervening years since publication of the earlier book.

Like the previous book, this one is offered as a guide to appropriate trading strategies. This one is also a work in progress in the sense that every trading system benefits from continual refinement. In recent years I have found important new information that serves to enhance trading success. This new information is potentially so useful that I have felt compelled to share it in this way. To the extent that the present book is successful, it will be a source of empowerment for many readers. However, I have made a conscious effort here to complement power with parsimony. In my own research my spreadsheets have grown to over a hundred columns with scores of variables producing reams of data for analysis and comparison. Here I have made every attempt to reduce the scope of the work to a minimum number of the most productive concepts. My hope is that the reader will embellish the work with additional channels of investigation that will be personally relevant, just as I too fully expect to find additional useful information in years to come. Given my age and stage, however, it is likely that this will be my last book on trading. Because of my growing interest in history and religion, it is probable that any of my future writing efforts will be focused in those areas. I am making this present work public because I do not want the years of effort represented here to be lost to those few serious persons who will want to take advantage of these findings.

One other comment is necessary here at the beginning of this work. Trading is an honorable occupation. It provides bread to the eater. If done properly, it should not be considered to be gambling any more than a farmer should be considered to be gambling when he plants his crops. Moreover, trading must not be considered anti-religious behavior. It is a longstanding fallacy to equate business success with crass materialism and selfish greed. In fact, for persons like me who are serious followers of Jesus Christ, trading provides an opportunity to fulfill the Lord's directive, "Actively trade until I come," (Luke 19:13, original Greek). Furthermore, a belief in creative design adds impetus to trading because it reinforces the view that natural phenomena such as market trends follow predictable patterns and are governed by rules just like other physical and behavioral phenomena in the cosmos. Religious faith is compatible with a view that market behavior constitutes a category of phenomena that is every bit as predictable as the weather.

Nor should trading activity be viewed as an alternative to work—indeed, it may involve more intensive labor than you are accustomed to—but it is a means of harnessing the beneficial elements of modern capitalism that have thanklessly contributed so much to our high standard of living. Capitalism as a system is not without its challenges, but it is clearly better than any alternatives that have presented themselves so far. However, the potential benefits of free-market capitalism have been greatly impeded in today's world. Remember that just as there is a profound difference between capitalism and socialism, so also there is a great chasm between capitalism and crony capitalism. Just as democracy is associated with the right to vote for the leadership we desire and thereby ensure personal liberty, so capitalism is associated with the right to own shares of publicly traded companies and thereby increase wealth. I believe that, to the extent that we have the privilege to exercise these rights, we also have the responsibility to do so.

At this time of serious problems in the international economy, including uncontrolled government spending with its concomitant red ink and rising private sector unemployment, I wish to offer encouraging information about a viable method of financial subsistence. My target audience includes recent university graduates who find themselves saddled with debt and unable to gain suitable employment, as well as retirees whose incomes are inadequate, and various members of a displaced work force who resent living on government subsidies. I hope also to demonstrate here that one does not need huge capital resources to benefit financially from market participation.

Of course there are financial hazards in equities trading that dictate that every trader must be circumspect. Few persons come away from the marketplace unscathed, and many of those who do are often unscathed because they are trading with other people's money (OPM). However, the old adage, "Nothing ventured, nothing gained," is just as appropriate today as it has been in earlier times. The very presence of apparent hazards often serves as a portent of undiscovered rewards. The complex gyrations and awesome rewards entailed in equities trading also present an enormous challenge to any enquiring mind with an inclination to problem solving. This is a ferocious chess game with huge benefits for the winners. Even so eminent a scholar and thinker as Albert Einstein is reported to have said that if he had it to do over again, he would become a stock operator instead of a physicist. As it happens, some of the world's keenest minds have already concentrated on the study of the intricacies of financial markets. If you are seeking a challenge, you have come to the right place. What you will read in the coming chapters constitutes this author's own best effort to meet that challenge.

INTRODUCTION

A Background Rationale for the Use of Mathematical Models in Stock Trading

Watching stock market fluctuations, the casual observer may conclude that the stock market is like a gigantic pot of alphabet soup boiling over a hot fire. Stocks, as their share prices increase, rise to the top for a few days or weeks, only to cool and sink back down into the pot. In their constant churning, the majority of stocks never even reach the top of the pot. Many observers of this boiling chaos have given up all hope of finding a reliable pattern of stock performance. They have been told that market activity is a "random walk" and near-term market participation is at best a risky gamble. Nobel laureate economists have demonstrated to the satisfaction of many in the academic community that the market is "efficient." This is interpreted to mean that any legal informational advantage to guide traders about price movement has already been priced into the market. In other words, non-zero risk-adjusted returns (RARs)—otherwise known as "anomalies" that represent profitable disequilibria in the market—rarely if ever exist. Of course, not everyone agrees with this dictum.

The joke has been told about a university finance professor of the strong efficient market school who was walking along the street one day with one of his graduate students. Together they spied a ten dollar bill lying on the sidewalk. When the student reached down to pick it up, the professor admonished him, "Don't bother. If it were a real ten dollar bill, someone would have picked it up by now." So it is that advocates of the strong version of the efficient market hypothesis miss a lot of good opportunities.

In the face of such chaos and confusion, it seems that serious market participants are of two main types. There are those investors who pick out a few stocks, funds, or indices of interest and buy them with the intention of holding them for many months or years. They are committed to those companies, funds or indices for various idiosyncratic reasons, and they do not ever intend to sell them until a compelling need to sell arises. Those investors are content to realize annual gains equal to or slightly above the gains of the major market indices. They are patient and have a long-term horizon. Because equity markets have had average annual returns of approximately seven percent, these investors are usually happy with that level of return. For that reason also they may even invest exclusively in index funds or reliable mutual funds through their retirement accounts and leave the serious decision-making to the professionals. Many "value" investors with large capital resources and comfortable retirement goals fit into this category. This approach makes very little demand on their time or their anxiety-tolerance levels. It also entails no great requirement for them to pay brokerage commissions or capital gains taxes. They have low expectations, and they often manage to reach those expectations. It may even be said that they are "risk averse."

An entirely different category of market participant includes many kinds of active traders. These persons also observe the same wild market fluctuations, but form vastly different conclusions about those fluctuations. They embrace risk as a viable opportunity for reward. They are not satisfied with nominal investment returns that barely keep pace with inflation. They view market participation as a treasure hunt, a warfare comprised of daily battles with commensurate spoils and losses, a search for alpha—the often elusive formula for consistent success–a chess match against an elusive grandmaster. They are convinced—whether by instinct, experience, research, or other empirical evidence—that the market is replete with anomalies (examples of predictable and profitable disequilibria) that can be exploited for financial gain. These anomalies include, but are not limited to, surprise earnings announcements, share buyback programs, directional momentum, price gaps up or down, disproportional insider ownership acquisitions, post-earnings-announcement drift, and a host of other examples such as those ably documented in Zacks (2011). However, these active traders soon discover that it is not possible to harness these anomalies to greatest benefit without the use of mathematical systems.

It should come as no surprise that this present author belongs to the latter camp. My background, however, is not in business or finance, but in psychometrics. This is not an apology, because cross-disciplinary research is often highly productive—a form of intellectual arbitrage. For many years it was my job to design and validate university entrance examinations. That explains why I approach the picking of stocks for inclusion into a portfolio rather like choosing students for admission to university. Because there is limited university classroom space, and because there are limited resources for purchasing stocks to enter a portfolio, the task reduces to one of defining a valid measurable criterion of selection, ranking the stocks or students in a reliable manner from first to last on the criterion, and deciding on a cut score for inclusion or rejection.

There are many challenges to be faced in this process. For example, it turns out that there are multiple valid measurement criteria that may be used for ranking–although some are more valid than others. This suggests that it can be useful to employ multiple ranking criteria simultaneously. It also happens that stocks—and probably students–frequently alter status on the ranking criteria. As with any predictive model, it also occurs that there are estimation errors, and these errors grow in magnitude as estimates are extended into the ever-increasing future using data drawn from the ever-increasing past. To explain by way of example, university entrance examination scores are not a useful indication of university potential if those scores are many months or years old at the time the student applies for admission. Also, even when current, they fail to predict academic success accurately beyond the first year or two in university. Nevertheless, if used correctly in a timely manner, they have great power in predicting university success and go far beyond what is possible with mere interviews or letters of recommendation. In the same way, mathematical models have great power for predicting future growth in stock prices, but only if the right variables have been chosen as predictors, and only if timely and accurate input data are used, and then only if predictions are not made too far into the future.

In the following chapters I have outlined a process whereby individual stocks can be ranked for probability of future growth. This is an attempt to bring dependable order into seeming chaos.

CHAPTER 1

DEFINING A PORTFOLIO DATABASE

> "And I set my heart to seek and search out wisdom concerning all that is done under heaven; this burdensome task God has given to the sons of man by which they may be exercised."
> — ECCLESIASTES 1:13

Every financial engineer (and probably every stock trader) needs a database comprised of requisite data on a current sample of select stocks. I remember the commencement address by the dean of my daughter's nursing school many years ago. She said that every nurse needs a patient database that will enable her to learn from her patients, improve the quality of her professional service, and also to overcome professional burnout. By extension, I believe that every teacher can also benefit from a student database that will help the teacher learn from her or his students and serve them better. Certainly equities traders need to maintain a database that will allow them to track stock performance, learn from market action, and make the best possible buying and selling decisions.

However, there are too many publicly traded equities (varying from 4,000 to 8,000, not counting many kinds of funds that offer combinations and permutations of stock offerings) to permit daily upgrading and analysis of them all in one large database. This is especially true since the objective here is to use detailed information to locate and employ the best predictive anomalies in order to rank all of the stocks in the database for purposes of investment at any given moment. Therefore, it is necessary to reduce the number of stocks under observation for purposes of analysis.

I start this streamlining process by making a list of all the publicly traded stocks listed on the NASDAQ, the NYSE, and the AMEX that have satisfied certain performance criteria over the past year. Specifically, I first look for those stocks that have gained more than 30 percent in the past three months. In principle, stocks that have moved sharply upward show upward momentum and have an increased probability of moving higher in the foreseeable future. To ensure that this upward momentum is still in place, I further eliminate all stocks that have not gained at least 10 percent in the past month, and all those stocks that are not priced within three percent of their 52-week highs. I have come to insist upon the 10-percent current-month criterion because I have a goal of realizing at least 10 percent gain in each trading month. Stocks that do not satisfy this criterion are unlikely to help me reach my trading goal. A stronger rationale for including the "0-3% below High" delimiter will be provided in the next chapter concerning "Percentage Lag." For now it is enough to say that this requirement is included to ensure that upward momentum is still intact and to reduce the portfolio database further to a manageable size. Happily all of these criteria can be satisfied at once by using a free online stock screener such as the one at www.Finviz.Com.

Simply go to that website, click on "Screener" and then click on "Technical." Under "Performance," enter "quarter+30%," and under "Performance2," enter "month +10%." Finally, under "52-Week High/Low" enter "0-3% below High." This should provide you with a list of from 15 to 50 stocks, depending on market conditions. If you follow this process at the close of trading each day and add any new stocks to your portfolio database, eventually your list should grow to a number approaching 100 stocks, depending again on market conditions. Note that this website has many other screening possibilities of a descriptive, fundamental, or technical nature that may provide you with years of exciting research opportunities. For now, it is best to focus only on the three performance criteria given above. More complexity will be added soon enough. Bear in mind that occasionally this process will identify stocks that are being acquired, and thus their share price has reached a plateau so that they should not be added to your portfolio. Also, do not ordinarily include exchange traded funds (ETFs) that may appear by screening, because it is not possible to get fundamental data for their evaluation. You can often find many additional stocks by going to www. Stockcharts.com and clicking on "Predefined Scan Results" on the home page and then looking for stocks making new 52-week highs. After selecting an exchange, you can click on the SCTR column heading and find those stocks in the 99th percentile ranking for technical characteristics. There also you can conveniently examine charts to decide whether to include stocks in your database for subsequent analysis.

At this point you are ready to begin entering your database information into an Excel spreadsheet or into some similar database management software. As shown in Table 1.1 below, use the first column for stock symbol, the second column for current share price, the third column for 52-week high, the fourth column for 52-week low, the fifth column for "multiple" (i.e., current price divided by low), and the sixth column for "%Lag" (i.e., high minus current price, the remainder divided by high). In terms of Excel software, you would make the following entry into cell E2 as shown in Table 1.1: =B2/D2. You would then copy cell E2, drag it down through all the rows in that column for which you have stocks in your database, and paste it there. Similarly, in cell F2 you would make the following entry: =(C2-B2)/C2. You would copy and paste it to the F column in the same way. All of these required entry data are readily available at the Yahoo Finance website, or at dozens of other websites. With Excel spreadsheets the formulas can be conveniently embedded in the cells and copied down the columns using the COPY and PASTE commands. Remember to round off entries to the nearest penny for ease of entry where applicable. Also, in those cases where a stock is currently priced exactly at its 52-week high, it may initially be necessary to enter its current price at one cent below that high for computational purposes because it is not possible to divide by zero in subsequent calculations. This last requirement may become unnecessary when the full spreadsheet is entered if you do not intend to use computations that would involve division by zero. Table 1.1 below presents actual sample data by using this procedure on May 26, 2014. Notice that the stocks have been ranked in ascending order according to %Lag in column F using the Excel SORT command.

TABLE 1.1. Twenty Stocks Arranged in Ascending Order for Proximity to New 52-Week Highs on May 26, 2014.

	A	B	C	D	E	F
	Symbol	Price	High	Low	Mult	%Lag
	PAH	25.37	25.38	11.75	2.16	4E04
	THRM	42.9	42.92	16.52	2.6	5E04
	PCYG	11.97	11.98	5.05	2.37	8E04
	FUR	15.05	15.09	10.77	1.4	0.003
	ITMN	39.98	40.13	9.27	4.31	0.004
	AMKR	9.53	9.57	3.91	2.44	0.004
	PPC	25.1	25.25	11.41	2.2	0.006
	ARX	10.53	10.6	6.04	1.74	0.007
	GBX	55.5	55.87	21.1	2.63	0.007
	DAVE	31.76	31.99	11.7	2.71	0.007
	SKX	42.45	43.04	19.99	2.12	0.014
	CXDC	10.06	10.2	3.99	2.52	0.014
	WFT	21.2	21.5	12.99	1.63	0.014
	ECOL	49.65	50.37	26.68	1.86	0.014
	TSYS	3.38	3.43	2.08	1.63	0.015
	IBN	51.46	52.28	24.94	2.06	0.016
	SLCA	49.44	50.26	19.26	2.57	0.016
	MACK	7.52	7.65	2.05	3.67	0.017
	DDS	109.77	111.74	75.6	1.45	0.018
	SWC	17.46	17.78	9.78	1.79	0.018

It will be immediately apparent to the reader that there is tremendous power available through maintaining a database in this way. You can easily sort the stocks according to any variable of interest, whether alphabetically by symbol, by share price, by the number of times the price has multiplied from the 52-week low, by proximity to new 52-week highs, or by any other variable that we will encounter in subsequent chapters. You can also perform endless statistical tests and manipulations of the data. Bear in mind, however, that these data will fluctuate from day to day so that most of these stocks will have changed position or disappeared from the list by the time you read this.

With these three delimiters (i.e., share price increasing at least 30% over one quarter, share price increasing at least 10 percent over the past month, and percentage lag of less than three percent from the 52-week high), we are able to define a manageable database as a starting point for subsequent analysis and decision making. At the end of each trading day, there is usually a changing of the guard; that is, several stocks will usually be dropped and replaced in the portfolio database. Stocks are eliminated from the database when it happens that they have no longer gained at least ten percent in the past month, or 30 percent over the past three months. In practice, I find it useful to combine the one-month and three-month requirements to require 40 percent combined. We shall see in the next chapter how easy it is to implement this procedure. It is not unusual for stocks that have been thus eliminated to rejoin the list after several months or years. The challenge is to hold stocks while they are rising in share price and to sell them when they are in decline. Other criteria for stock deletion may also be used, such as deleting all stocks that are more than 15 percentage points below their 52-week highs (as will be evident in column F), or deleting all stocks that have multiplied less than 1.6 times from their 52-week lows to their current stock price (as will be evident in column E)

Maintaining this updated portfolio database is the most challenging and time-consuming part of trading by the numbers. It requires daily share-price updating for all stocks and fresh inputting of all relevant statistical data for at least the top half of the database. Because I do this manually, it requires an hour or two at the end of each trading day. But the payoff is huge. I am able thereby to rank-order all of the stocks in the database on more than a dozen indexed criteria of suitability for purchase or sale. In terms of measurement theory, I am able to define a valid "latent trait" of prospective profitability. It greatly removes the guesswork from stock trading. I am able to conduct statistical research regarding any quantifiable variables to capture anomalies and capitalize on market disequilibria. Although it may be considered to be hard work, it is every bit as enjoyable as cultivating, planting, and maintaining a garden and watching the produce materialize over time. It may seem onerous at the outset, but it is a small price to pay to ensure the possibility of monthly gains in excess of ten percent. The good news for you is that I have streamlined this process in the present work so that you may be able to make all necessary updates in approximately 45 minutes at the close of trading each day. And of course it is not necessary to implement every component of the trading system described here, so that you can reduce the time commitment even more.

Summary:

In this chapter we have considered the importance of maintaining a portfolio database to permit analysis and selection or rejection of stocks for inclusion into an actual portfolio. You can begin this process by opening your Excel spreadsheet and creating six initial columns. The first column can be labeled *SYMBOL*, for it will contain the ticker symbols of all of the stocks of interest to you. You can label the second column *PRICE*, for it will contain the current share prices of all of the stocks in your list. The next four columns can be labeled *HIGH, LOW, MULTIPLE,* and *%LAG*, as shown in Table 1.1 above.

One quick way to identify stocks for entry into your database is to use an online stock screener such as the one at *Finviz.Com*. If you go to the home page of *Finviz.Com* and click on the tab *Screener* and then click on the tab *Technical,* you will be ready to begin your search. In the *Performance* category in the upper left-hand corner you should scroll down to *Quarter+30%*. This will select all of the stocks that have grown at least 30 percent in price over the past three months. Next move right to the *Performance* 2 category and scroll down to *Month +10%*. This will further delimit your list to include only those stocks that have gained 10 percent or more in the past month. Finally, move to the *52-Week High/Low* category in the center. Scroll down to *0-3% below High,* and your list of stocks will be further delimited to those that are within three percent of their 52-week highs. Depending on market conditions, you should now have a list of about 20 stocks at the bottom of the web page. 20 Stocks are enough to begin operations on a manageable scale. It is good to start small. At the end of each trading day you will need to repeat this process and possibly also examine all stocks making new 52-week highs.

Eventually your database should grow to about 70 to 120 stocks, depending on market conditions.

Once your database reaches this desirable size, you may simplify the selection process somewhat by choosing stocks that have gained 20 percent in the last month and eliminating the criterion of 30 percent gain over the past three months.

PART ONE

Technicals

Technical concerns for stock selection include patterns of price movement that portend future price movement. True technicians tend to believe that technical data reflect psychological behaviors of market participants and thus indirectly incorporate all that is known about stock fundamentals and provide sufficient information to predict future price movement without the need to specifically reference fundamental stock data. The following five chapters address several technical anomalies that are known to be predictive of future price movement. Part Two of this book will address fundamental concerns in the belief that fundamentals are also important. While both technical and fundamental influences are critically important, technical influences tend to be more immediate and ephemeral and fundamental influences more gradual and lasting.

CHAPTER 2

Percentage Lag (Proximity to New Highs)

> "I made myself water pools from which to
> water the growing trees of the grove."
> — Ecclesiastes 2:6

Here, what I term "percentage lag" is a measure of share-price proximity to new highs. This is arguably the most important technical variable in equities trading. The rationale for this assertion is simply that every good stock should eventually reach new highs in share price, and it is precisely at the time that new highs are being registered that the stock becomes most attractive to the investment community. This is one facet of price momentum that is easily detected. It has been argued elsewhere that about 70 percent of stocks making new highs go on to make additional new highs. A river shows acceleration of its current as it approaches a waterfall. In the same way, a stock tends to show increased trading volume and upward momentum as it approaches new highs in price.

Another nice thing about percentage lag is that it is a performance criterion that does not lie. Analyst ratings, sales forecasts, price targets, and earnings projections are subjectively determined and thus can easily be inaccurate—and frequently can be intentionally distorted. But percentage lag cannot be fudged. For this reason it can serve as a reality check. By using the Excel "sort" function, you now can easily rank-order all of the stocks in your portfolio by proximity to new highs. If you had no other indicators of future share-price gain, you could still trade profitably using this percentage-lag ranking. To take advantage of the percentage-lag statistic in actual trading, you will need to incorporate a rule of thumb. For example, I usually never buy a stock that is more than two percentage points below its 52-week high. Stocks already in your portfolio that drop below four percentage points from their 52-week highs are considered to be stocks that should be sold unless there are extenuating circumstances that dictate that they should be held longer. One such extenuating circumstance is "same-day purchase." Because I do not wish to become a day trader, I try to avoid selling stocks on the same day that they are purchased. Similarly, stocks that drop more than five percent below their 52-week highs are considered to be stocks that must be sold, unless there are likewise extenuating circumstances. Of course, there are other profitable strategies that involve "bottom fishing," that consist of buying stocks that have bottomed in price, but such strategies are not included in the repertoire of strategies recommended in this book. And that omission is intentional, due in part to my belief that stocks rising from a steep bottom require longer in their ascent to overcome the "overhang" due to holders of the stock who bought in earlier at a higher than current price.

Keeping track of percentage lag for a portfolio of stocks requires the daily updating of the first few columns in your Excel spreadsheet or other data management software. In chapter one you learned how to create a portfolio database with six initial columns on your spreadsheet as shown in Table 1.1. In that table percentage lag was listed as the final column on the right. The percentage lag column is obtained by subtracting the current share prices from their 52-week highs and dividing the remainders with the same 52-week share prices. You do this by entering a formula in the top data cell of the *%Lag* column by using the = sign. You then copy this cell, drag it down, and paste it through all of the rows for which you have stocks in your database. It is usually safe to limit focus to this 52-week window. This is because companies change so dramatically in management, business model, profitability, market capitalization, and future prospects within a 52-week period that they are often tantamount to new companies altogether by comparison with their status more than a year ago.

Some clever graduate student will write to tell me that what I call "percentage lag" is not really a percentage at all, but is a proportion. That is true, but "percentage lag" sounds much better than "proportional lag," and anyone so inclined can multiply by 100 to convert the proportions to percentages. The basic message of this chapter is that proximity to new highs is an extremely important variable. It has the power to identify stocks that are moving up in price with momentum, and it can serve as a safety valve—an indication of time to sell.

At the same time, buying and selling stocks within a five percentage-point window of their 52-week highs may result in a very high turnover rate in your portfolio. This certainly has negative implications for commission expenditures and for tax liabilities. Nevertheless, I find that the value of acquiring stocks that are moving rapidly upward in price and the protection afforded by avoiding catastrophic losses from price declines below five percent, more than compensate for commissions and taxes—especially if you trade online with commissions of seven dollars or less per trade. Traders will, however, need to establish their own boundaries within which they can maintain comfort and experience profitability.

Evaluation and Summary:

In this chapter I have asserted that a trader could trade profitably using no other information about stocks than their proximities to new highs. To test that assertion, on September 26, 2013, I selected an exhaustive sample of the 20 stocks closest to their 52-week highs from among all of those stocks on the NYSE, Nasdaq, and AMEX that had doubled in price in the past year, and I constructed an experimental $20,000.00 portfolio with an equal $1000.00 invested in each of those stocks. (For the record, those stocks were ALNY, ALU, ARWR, BREW, CLDX, CMLS, CNTY, CTCT, CTRP, DWCH, DYAX, FB, ICEL, ICPT, IGTE, LCI, NUS, SPA, TASR, and TSLA.) On January 14, 2014 (exactly four months later) that portfolio had increased in value from $20,000.00 to $26,076.41–a gain of 30.38 percent, which is a very respectable gain within a four-month period. During the same period, the S&P500 Index climbed from 1698.67 to 1790.29—a gain of only 5.39 percent. The percentage lag portfolio outperformed the S&P500 by nearly six times! Bear in mind that this is a conservative evaluation exercise for two reasons. First, most sane persons would not continue to hold any losing stocks in their portfolios for four months despite discouraging news and plummeting share price on the part of any one stock, and second, most savvy traders would not put as many as 20 stocks in their portfolios by any single criterion. They would also realize that such an abundance of stocks would only tend to approximate the performance of the major indices. Instead they would likely select at most only the top five or ten stocks by any one criterion. Admittedly, the sample was limited not only to the stocks closest to their 52-week highs, but also included only stocks that had already doubled in price over the past year. At that particular time the only stocks in my database portfolio were those that had doubled in price over the past year.

When you consider the predictive power of just this single technical variable "percentage lag," you will not be surprised to see in subsequent chapters the extent to which performance may be enhanced still further by taking this variable in combination with other successful technical and fundamental predictor variables. You will see that a central message of this book is how to explain the variance in equity performance by constructing mathematical models with variables entered into an Excel spreadsheet. This is not only a demonstration that stock performance is not random, but it is solid evidence that you can make accurate predictions about future equity performance and can successfully capitalize on those predictions in the same way that meteorologists can forecast changes in the weather. This constitutes evidence that, as Albert Einstein has said, "God is not playing dice with his universe."

CHAPTER 3

Momentum

> "The end of a thing is better than its beginning; the
> patient in spirit is better than the proud in spirit."
> — Ecclesiastes 7.8

There is a large body of research evidence supporting the view that momentum is perhaps the most dependable source of market disequilibria (Zacks, 2011). Whenever it is observed that a stock is regularly making new highs in price, increasing in daily trading volume, and growing in market capitalization, a lot of investor interest is aroused. Traders and investors alike tend to pile onto that stock and propel it to yet higher highs—often beyond all rational valuation of the stock. There is a kind of crowd psychology at play that creates a variety of "self-fulfilling prophecy." This psychological phenomenon can be seen both in positive upward momentum of share prices and in negative downward momentum of share prices. Thus, for a time stocks are said to become "overbought" or "oversold." For a momentum trader, "overbought" or "oversold" conditions are not a problem, so long as the momentum is still moving in the desired direction. There are many ways to measure momentum. The problem for the trader is how best to measure momentum for purposes of guiding trading decisions.

In a sense, by selecting a database comprised of stocks that have risen at least 30 percent in the past quarter, 10 percent in the past month, and that are within three percent of their 52-week highs, we have already captured some of what is intended by momentum. Over many months and years of market watching, however, I have observed that merely selecting a database with stocks that have increased in price by at least 30 percent in the past quarter and 10 percent over the past month, and further eliminating stocks with greater than three percent lag from their 52-week highs does not sufficiently identify stocks with upward price momentum, nor does it provide us with a quantitative index of momentum.

Moreover, momentum is a range-bound concept. That is to say, momentum may persist for only a week, a month, a quarter, a year, or up to several years. To be useful for purposes of trading, the longer momentum persists, the better. In order to take into consideration the ephemeral nature of momentum, it is best to measure it within differing periods of duration. With that in mind, I look at momentum within a short-term period of one month, within a long-term period of twelve months, and for purposes of reliability of measurement I combine the two measurements to come up with a cumulative measure of momentum.

At this point it will be productive to add new information to your Excel spreadsheet so that you can routinely generate momentum indices for ranking stocks in your database.

TABLE 3.1. Twenty Stocks Arranged in Descending Order for Cumulative Momentum (CMI) on June 7, 2014

A	G	H	I	J	K	L	M	N
Symbol	1MoPr	3MoPr	1MoGn	3MoGn	ToGn	1MM	12MM	CMI
GMK	37.59	33.08	18.542	34.704	53.246	18.318	746.4	764.72
PAM	7.67	4.8	22.816	96.25	119.07	20.698	108.81	129.51
PL	51.24	52.49	35.558	32.33	67.888	34.264	70.349	104.61
HSH	35.3	37.52	66.912	57.036	123.95	57.664	10.179	67.842
MMI	15.73	17.49	42.975	28.588	71.563	40.314	26.989	67.303
CXDC	6.83	5.09	78.624	139.69	218.31	56.188	9.1712	65.359
ITMN	30.83	13.77	33.441	198.77	232.21	24.767	39.358	64.124
SSLT	11.91	11.82	74.307	75.635	149.94	46.217	5.7363	51.954
DAVE	26.79	25.58	28.331	34.402	62.733	21.399	26.527	47.926
SKX	41.12	34.63	15.175	36.76	51.935	11.598	34.178	45.776
ENG	2.1	1.58	82.857	143.04	225.9	33.352	8.9051	42.257
IDCC	34.26	31.5	37.069	49.079	86.149	28.624	9.3412	37.965
PES	14.97	11.52	9.5524	42.361	51.914	4.6981	31.697	36.395
NFX	31.83	28.19	17.122	32.245	49.368	13.381	18.257	31.638
BBW	11.93	8.25	27.913	84.97	112.88	16.895	13.855	30.75
SAIA	38.1	34.23	19.318	32.807	52.125	15.155	15.547	30.703
PHX	43.15	38.28	34.739	51.881	86.62	21.501	8.5511	30.052
SNDK	86.26	75.45	15.94	32.551	48.492	11.164	18.502	29.666
DYN	28.45	23.03	22.882	51.802	74.684	14.655	11.309	25.965
ENSG	22.12	23.03	38.969	33.478	72.447	20.137	3.3038	23.441

Notice in Table 3.1 that eight new columns of data (G through N) have been added to the columns (A through F) listed in Table 1.1. For ease of representation, columns B through F are not shown in this new table. Column G records the price of each stock exactly one month prior to June 7, 2014. Column H records the price of each stock exactly three months before that same date. Normally we record this information from today's date. You can find this information at many websites. I like to use the interactive charts at Yahoo Finance for each stock, click on the one-month and two-month charts, and move the cursor to the far left to obtain the required pricing information. Once you have taken the time and trouble to enter the vital information in columns A through H, all of the technical information necessary to rank stocks and inform trading decisions can be generated routinely by your computer.

As you can see in Table 3.1, column I contains one-month gain for each of the stocks in the database. This is the percentage increase each stock has made over the past month. It is obtained by dividing the difference between current price and one-month's prior price by the amount of the one month's prior price, and multiplying the result times 100. The Excel formula to be entered into cell I2 and dragged down the column is as follows: =(B2-I2)/I2*100. Three-month percentage gain is found in column J and is promulgated by the following formula: =(B2-J2)/J2*100. Column K contains total percentage gain and reports the sum of columns I and J using the following formula: =I2+J2. Column K becomes especially useful at the end of each trading day when it becomes possible to sort stocks on total percentage gain from the largest to smallest and to cull out any stocks that have fallen out of favor by dropping below the sum of 40.

So far we have arrived at not only percentage lag of each stock from its 52-week high, but we now also have percentage gains of each stock over both one-month and three-month intervals. The next steps will be to compute one-month, twelve-month, and combined one-plus-twelve month momentum indices for each stock. This information is reported in columns L through N in Table 3.1 above. In column L we use the following formula to generate one-month momentum: =I2-(500*F2). This formula is entered into cell L2, copied, and dragged down the column as in the earlier examples. The formula for twelve-month momentum to be entered into cell M2 is as follows: =(((B2-D2)/D2)*100)-(2000*F2). This formula is then copied and dragged down the M column in the same way. Note that by using adaptations of this formula, you can measure momentum both positively and negatively within any time interval you may choose.

As you inspect the formulae in columns L and M, you can see that momentum is here defined operationally in its respective intervals as a combination of rate of growth and proximity to new highs. Momentum declines or becomes negative as the stock price ceases to increase and departs from its 52-week high. You will observe that momentum defined in this way can be highly volatile—especially in its one-month representation. For this reason it is useful to combine columns L and M to derive a cumulative momentum index (CMI) as reported in column N of Table 3.1. The formula entered in cell N2 for arriving at this final index is as follows: =L2+M2. This also is copied and dragged down the N column as we saw before.

Momentum traders may find it profitable to base trades exclusively on the one month momentum index in column L. This index effectively identifies the hottest stocks in your database at any given moment. It also alerts you to sell stocks when momentum turns negative. This author relies heavily on this index in both bullish and bearish market conditions.

The beauty of the Excel spreadsheet is that it allows you to rank order all of your stocks by momentum within any interval of interest by simply using the SORT command. This has been done for you with regard to the CMI in Table 3.1. It is often instructive to compare the one-month and twelve-month momentum indexes. Notice, for example that on June 7th, 2014, the twelve-month momentum in column M for the stock GMK was much higher than for the stock HSH; but the relative momentum strength for those two stocks was reversed in the one-month interval reported in column L. Interestingly, HSH went on to surpass GMK in relative price gains for a while in the ensuing period.

Summary:

In this chapter we have seen how to enter stock prices from the previous one-month and three-month points in time and to use that information to promulgate indices of percentage gain and cumulative momentum for purposes of ranking stocks in your database. We have considered the ephemeral nature of momentum and have seen how it is possible to rank stocks for momentum within various time intervals. It has been suggested in this chapter that momentum provides a powerful technical indicator of probability of stock price gain in the near term. When taken alongside of percentage lag as described in Chapter Two, the predictive technical anomaly to be presented in this book that attempts to capture the predictive value of patterns of price movement.

CHAPTER 4

PRICE-ACTION RANKING

> "In the day of prosperity be joyful, but in the day of adversity consider; surely God has appointed the one as well as the other."
> — ECCLESIASTES 7:14

In the introduction to Part One of this book it was asserted that technical trading involves relying on patterns of price movement to make judgments about future price movement without a perceived need to take fundamentals into consideration. Technicians speak in terms of "head-and-shoulders" formations or "Elliott Wave Theory" cycles or other charting formations that are usually impossible to quantify in any systematic way. Too often those patterns are subjectively determined and do not lend themselves to comparative quantification or measurement. Therefore they are often not falsifiable in any scientific hypothesis-testing sense. What I am attempting to do in this chapter is to provide such quantification—at least to the extent that it can become a basis for the rank-ordering of stocks on desirability for acquisition.

I pause here briefly to reflect that what you are about to add to your spreadsheet is the end result of years of research involving much trial and error and many trading failures and successes. What I have attempted to do here is to derive a mathematical curve-fitting algorithm that allows you to rank stocks in terms of an actual price-movement function. I arrived at this procedure inductively, attempting to find relationships predictive of one-month growth in share prices. I examined many variables and their combinations and permutations for their power to predict this one-month growth in share price. Perhaps because of my experience in the validation of university entrance examinations I have been hesitant to look beyond one month—forward or backward–for predictive power. I know from subsequent experience that the resulting Price Movement Index (PMI) provides powerful prediction of future price movement; however, I cannot fully explain why it works, any more than Thomas Edison could provide some "molecular illumination theory" to explain why his discovery of tungsten filament allowed him to produce incandescent lighting. It was a serendipitous pragmatic discovery that was the end result of a lot of hard work through trial and error. But all he knew for sure was that tungsten worked to produce light; whereas, other elements had failed.

In order to promulgate the Price Movement Index (PMI) it will be necessary to add two more columns to the spreadsheet you have already constructed. The two new columns O and P are shown by example at the far right side of Table 4.1. Notice in this table that columns C, D, K, L, M, and N have been purposely deleted just to enable the table to fit on the page. Also, the entries in those columns are not directly employed in the computation of the PMI. Because the formula for the computation of the PMI is lengthy, Column O labeled "Num" is merely a portion of the numerator on one side of the equation that is entered in this way for convenience. The computation requires two stages.

TABLE 4.1. Twenty Stocks Arranged in Descending Order on the Price Movement Index (PMI) on June 20, 2014.

A	B	E	F	G	H	I	J	O	P
Symbol	Price	Mult	%Lag	1MoPr	3MoPr	1MoGn	3MoGn	Num	PMI
NZ	5.41	2.76	0.022	3.63	4.25	49.036	27.294	4.6815	41.4
SYNA	91.35	2.61	5E04	57.74	61.48	58.209	48.585	5.5116	33
VNCE	37.65	1.67	0.009	24.62	26.63	52.924	41.382	4.0592	25.68
SN	38	1.86	5E04	27.69	28.1	37.234	35.231	4.6559	24.59
RH	90.2	1.65	0.002	62.84	64.78	43.539	39.241	4.3119	23.85
WLB	36.66	3.4	0.012	27.75	26.64	32.108	37.613	5.6561	23.79
AMOT	16.22	2.44	0.016	12.2	12.24	32.951	32.516	4.6294	22.98
CSCD	13.63	2.1	0.012	9.91	10.01	37.538	36.164	4.4212	22.58
BDSI	12.4	3.21	0.032	8.96	8.88	38.393	39.64	4.6561	21.59
GRH	1.81	2.41	0.032	0.97	1.02	86.598	77.451	4.0333	21.59
REX	79.38	2.97	0.019	57.38	55.08	38.341	44.118	4.9828	21.09
BLUE	40.71	2.39	0.025	27.21	26.83	49.614	51.733	4.2447	19.61
CRZO	68.25	2.54	0.004	56.11	52.23	21.636	30.672	5.2592	18.43
RMBS	14.69	1.85	0.001	11.32	10.61	29.77	38.454	4.599	17.76
LNG	68.54	2.74	0.012	57.4	53.68	19.408	27.683	5.0501	17.33
CODE	21.41	2.21	0.034	17.91	17.72	19.542	20.824	3.8065	16.85
AXDX	29.33	4.28	0.006	22.71	18.1	29.15	62.044	6.7045	15.58
GLNG	56.49	1.85	0.023	43.59	40.85	29.594	38.286	3.8041	14.02
FANG	89.79	2.92	0.038	71.15	65.68	26.198	36.708	4.2478	14.02
TWTC	40.83	1.58	0.02	32.73	31.16	24.748	31.033	3.5882	13.7

The Excel formula to be entered into cell O2 for the first stage computation is as follows: =SQRT(1.5*E2)/(5*(F2+0.1))*1.4. After entering this formula in cell O2, you will need to copy and drag the formula down the O column as you have done previously. You can see so far that the computation involves a weighted combination of percentage lag and the number of times in the past 52 weeks the share price has multiplied off its low. This takes advantage of yearly momentum as it has been defined here.

The second and final stage of the computation requires the following Excel formula to be entered into cell P2: =O2*I2/J2*5-5*F2. This formula in turn must be copied and dragged down the P column in the same way as the previous formula entries. You can see that this formula brings forward the computations entered in column O and incorporates information about one-month and three-month share price gain. The final values appearing in column P represent the Price Movement Index (PMI) which is the most powerful single predictor of share price gain that you have encountered in this book so far. Stocks that are highest on this index are the stocks most likely to rise in price in the near term, other considerations being equal. You can see in application that the actual patterns of share-price movement over the past one-month and three-month intervals will dictate the magnitude of the PMI.

Because the PMI is a function of current share price, 52-week high and low, and share price one month and three months earlier, it is necessary to input all of this information for every stock in your spreadsheet each day at the close of trading to derive an accurate calculation of the PMI for the market opening of the following day. This process is somewhat labor intensive, but it is well worth the effort.

Summary:

In this chapter we have seen how it is possible to compute a Price Movement Index (PMI) for the purpose of ranking stocks on their technical price movement patterns over the past year. The formula for this index was developed by comparing numerous alternative formulas for their power to predict one-month price movement. It was suggested that this index can be used as a portent of the likelihood that individual stocks will rise or fall in share price in the near future in the same way that technicians typically employ patterns such as those provided by "head and shoulders" formations, "Elliott Wave Theory," and "Bollinger Bands." In the next chapter we will see how this powerful prediction variable can be used to generate regression residuals that can allow us to rank stocks according to the magnitudes of their "outperforming" and "under-performing" conditions.

CHAPTER 5

REGRESSION RESIDUALS

> "If the ax is dull, and one does not sharpen the edge, then he must use more strength; but wisdom brings success."
> — ECCLESIASTES 10:10

Those of you who are familiar with regression analysis will know that, if two variables are correlated strongly enough, it is possible to predict or estimate values in one variable from corresponding values in the other variable. For example, suppose a person's weight is related to a person's height—which it is in fact. Therefore, if we know a person's height, we should be able to estimate that person's weight. There will of course be some errors of estimation—sometimes we may overestimate or underestimate the true weight of an individual when the estimation is based only on knowledge of that person's height. This is because some people are surprisingly light or surprisingly heavy for any given height. However, the expected amount of estimation error may itself even be quantified. Those errors of estimation for each person are known as residuals. If a person's weight exceeds his predicted weight by a specified amount based on that person's height, the residual might serve as a useful indication of obesity. In that case, subtracting the predicted weight from the actual weight would produce a positive remainder as a residual.

In the case of equities, if we have a variable that is sufficiently correlated with one-month share-price gain, then it is possible to estimate one-month share-price gain with a quantifiable degree of confidence.

If it is found that our estimate underestimated actual one-month share-price gain, we can reason that the stock has gained more than the amount that was expected and is therefore an "outperforming" stock by comparison with what market conditions might lead us to expect. The degree of overestimation or underestimation for each stock is expressed as a residual. Initially I equated an "outperforming" condition with an "overbought" condition, but subsequent observation has revealed that outperforming stocks may be expected to continue outperforming. We can expect such stocks to continue to gain in price over the near term because they have "room to run." Using the analogy of weight estimation, we can say that our finding of obesity does not suggest that immediate weight loss is impending. Rather, apart from some unusual intervention, we can expect weight gain to continue as usual. Of course with regard to equities, surprise news reports can always intervene to distort predictions, but in general we can use positive residuals in our search for outperforming stocks.

Note that Figure 5.1 below illustrates the typical relationship between one-month percentage gain shown on the vertical axis and the price movement index (PMI) score on the horizontal axis. The actual prices of individual stocks at a particular point in time are plotted with asterisks (*) in relation to the diagonal regression line. Those stocks that are located above the regression line are ones whose one-month gain has been underestimated by the regression equation. The stocks located below the regression line have had their one-month gain overestimated. The short perpendicular line that has been inserted for one stock below the regression line depicts the shortest distance from the stock to the regression line. The regression line is actually positioned amongst the stocks in such a way that the sum of the squares of all of the shortest distance lines is the smallest possible number. For that reason, the regression line is sometimes called "the line of best fit." A vertical line (not a perpendicular line) from any stock to the regression line marks the amount of deviation of that stock's actual one-month percentage gain from its estimated gain that is located on the regression line, which is what we call the "residual." In the case of the stock with the arrow in the figure, the residual is negative in value because the stock is located below the regression line and the remainder from subtracting the estimated stock price from the actual stock price will be a negative quantity.

Figure 5.1. Scattergram of Stocks Plotted in Relation to a Sample Regression Line Depicting the Relationship between One-Month Percentage Gain and PMI Score, with a Perpendicular Distance Line Inserted.

Stocks located above the regression line are of particular interest to the trader because they have exceeded their predicted potential and are shown to be "outperformers"; whereas, stocks located below the regression line have lagged behind prediction and may thus be considered to be "underperformers." Because this procedure allows us to quantify the actual estimated amount that a stock may be said to be over-performing or under-performing, you can readily imagine that it is potentially valuable and powerful. However, there are a few caveats to be remembered.

First of all, if the correlation between the variables of interest is not significant and meaningful, it is not possible to construct a useful regression line. The correlations observed between one-month share-price percentage gain and the Price Movement Index have consistently ranged between 0.4 and 0.7, which is adequate for this purpose—especially when it is considered that our sample has been truncated in that stocks with small or negative gains have already been eliminated. As a result, observed correlational magnitudes tend to be artificially conservative with this sample. However, whenever the correlation between one month gain and the price movement index (PMI) drops below .3, the residual is no longer helpful. This makes it necessary to compute the correlation of interest at the end of each trading day, which I do in an area on the extreme right-hand side of my spreadsheet.

In the second place, in spite of the fact that the scholarly financial literature is replete with Pearson product-moment correlations (I often am compelled to use them myself), such parametric statistics involving stock market data are highly unstable and suspect. That is because parametric statistics assume that the individual observations are normally and independently distributed. In the case of share-price gains, we know that they are not normally and independently distributed. Normality assumptions can still be satisfied through normalization transformations, but independence assumptions are not so easily satisfied. When the market rises, it lifts the majority of stock prices—a rising tide lifts all boats—and when the market falls, most stocks also decline in value. So gains and losses of individual stocks are not generally independent of gains and losses of other stocks. Happily this problem does not persist in other social sciences, and it does not affect correlations between student aptitude and achievement used for decisions about university admission. Although I do make limited application of correlation and regression at this one important point in this book, you will see that reliance is placed primarily on non-parametric rank statistics throughout the remainder of the book.

TABLE 5.1. Twenty Stocks Arranged in Descending Order of Positive Residuals in the Estimation of One-Month Growth on June 25, 2014.

A	B	C	D	E	F	G	I	P	Q	R
Symbol	Price	High	Low	Mult	%Lag	1MoPr	1MoGn	PMI	E1MGn	Resid
SYPR	5.86	6.5	2.52	2.33	0.098	2.95	98.644	9.02	26.7	71.94
GRH	1.88	2.03	0.75	2.51	0.074	0.99	89.899	12.12	23.04	66.86
BLUE	39.41	41.75	17.03	2.31	0.056	23.35	68.779	13.33	21.61	47.17
OMER	17.53	18.01	4.75	3.69	0.027	11.55	51.775	23.87	9.173	42.6
RH	92.37	93.54	54.61	1.69	0.013	66.08	39.785	27.38	5.034	34.75
GWPH	96.14	97.64	8.5	11.3	0.015	68.76	39.82	27.12	5.337	34.48
GLOG	31.65	32.44	12.56	2.52	0.024	23.14	36.776	22.03	11.35	25.43
LOAN	3.31	3.33	1.42	2.33	0.006	2.36	40.254	14.43	20.31	19.94
TAT	11.08	11.53	6.7	1.65	0.039	8.21	34.957	17.76	16.39	18.57
MMI	25.75	26.64	13.09	1.97	0.033	18.41	39.87	12.94	22.08	17.79
MMYT	34.25	34.91	13.02	2.63	0.019	25.94	32.035	19.27	14.6	17.43
SSLT	19.14	21.36	7.95	2.41	0.104	12.98	47.458	6.021	30.24	17.21
MARK	8.7	9.11	2.24	3.88	0.045	6.27	38.756	12.87	22.16	16.59
FOLD	3.03	3.1	1.77	1.71	0.023	2.21	37.104	13.32	21.63	15.47
BFR	11.8	12.08	3.61	3.27	0.023	8.9	32.584	17.12	17.14	15.44
MVG	9.46	10.64	4.87	1.94	0.111	6.96	35.92	12.05	23.13	12.79
VNCE	35.54	38	22.53	1.58	0.065	25.88	37.326	9.176	26.52	10.81
EDAP	4.44	4.52	2.38	1.87	0.018	3.31	34.139	11.64	23.6	10.54
IDCC	47.31	49.1	26.25	1.8	0.036	35.3	34.023	10.36	25.12	8.906
SYNA	89.38	91.5	37.87	2.36	0.023	67.78	31.868	12.03	23.15	8.715

Notice in Table 5.1 that once again several irrelevant columns (H, J, K, L, M, N, and O) have been removed to provide space to report on one page the information that is germane to the computation of residuals. The actual computation of residuals reported in column R at the far right side of the table requires three steps. First we must compute the correlation between one-month percentage gain reported in column I and the price movement index (PMI) reported in column P. Second we must compute the regression estimates of one-month percentage gain reported in column Q (E1MGn) that is based on the correlation. Third we must compute the residuals in column R by subtracting the estimated one-month gains in column Q from the actual one-month gains reported in column I.

Because we are trying to predict one-month share-price gain, we first try to identify the variable that has the highest and most stable correlation with one-month share-price gain. That variable turns out to be the

Price Movement Index in column P. That has been found to correlate consistently from 0.40 to 0.70 with one-month share-price gain, in spite of the truncation resulting from eliminating stocks with low or negative gains. In my own larger database I have found correlates of one-month share-price gain that range in magnitude from 0.60 to 0.80, but adding them to this book would definitely defeat our goal of parsimony. In a subsequent chapter, however, we will be introduced to an adjusted Price Movement Index (APMI) that frequently shows even higher correlation with one-month share-price gain.

In our present example reported in Table 5.1 the correlation coefficient is computed in a vacant cell to the right of the columns of your spreadsheet using the following formula: =CORREL(I2:I91, P2:P91). Note that CORREL is the Excel command for correlation, the correlation requested is between column I and column P (i.e. between one-month percentage gain and the Price Movement Index), and there happened to be 91 cases because there were 91 stocks in this database at the time of this computation. The resulting correlation coefficient was 0.414. Later I will show you how the correlation will increase when use is made of the APMI in the next chapter. As you add or remove stocks from the database at the end of each trading day, you will need to update the correlation and residual computations.

Using this correlation coefficient, we can now compute the regression estimates of one-month share-price gain reported in column Q. To do this we enter the following regression formula into cell Q2 and copy and drag it down the column: =0.414*(STDEV($I$2:$I$91)/STDEV($P$2:$P$91))*(P2-AVERAGE($P$2:$P$91)+AVERAGE($I$2:$I$91). Note that there should be no spaces in this entry. Note also that the dollar sign ($) is used so that Excel will hold the range values constant when you copy and drag the formula down column Q. As a result, column Q now reports the expected one-month share-price percentage gains as estimated by the regression formula.

Because we now have both the actual one-month share-price gains reported in column I and the estimated one-month share-price gains reported in column Q, we can compute the residuals by simply subtracting column Q entries from column I entries. To do this we enter the following formula into cell R2 and copy and drag it down column R: =I2-Q2.

Voila! We now have the residuals from the estimation of share-price gain arrayed in column R, and those stocks have been sorted in descending order with highest values at the top of the column. High positive values in column R tell us that the associated stocks have outperformed their estimates and have therefore become desirable for acquisition—other factors being equal. By simply using the Excel *SORT* command we could reverse the ordering of the stocks in column R of Table 5.1 and place the underperforming stocks at the top of the column. As you can readily imagine, residuals can become highly useful technical indicators.

I suspect that an entire book could be written just about the concepts of "over-performing" and "under-performing" equities and their relation to the concepts of "overbought" and "oversold." In the context of the present book what is meant by "over-performing" is that the price of the stock has risen beyond expectation given the relationships observed among predictive variables and underlying stocks. Similarly, "under-performing" means that the stock price has fallen below expectation. These conditions do bear some probability implications about future directions of a given stock. However, a stock that is said to be "over-performing" is not necessarily a bad investment. It may be that the factors that have caused the stock price to exceed expectation are persistent factors, and the stock may continue to exceed expectation. Earlier I used the example of obesity as an instance of exceeding expected weight given known height information. The existence of obesity does not imply impending weight loss. In fact, apart from unusual intervention, obesity may be expected to continue and increase. In the same way, over-performing stocks may be found to continue their over-performance.

Two complicating factors remain in the application of residuals that will be resolved in a later chapter. The first complication relates to the fact that market trends can affect the absolute magnitudes of the residual estimates. Thus, in a sharp market downtrend most stocks will appear to outpace estimates, and in a sharp uptrend stocks will appear to lag behind estimates. The solution to this problem that will be presented later is simply to convert residual estimates to ranks. This allows us to derive accurate comparative information on all stocks in our database regardless of market trends.

The second complication to be resolved may sometimes require a more stable correlate of one-month share-price gains than we have in the price movement index (PMI). It will be shown later that, despite the great usefulness of the PMI as a technical indicator, it can at times be distorted by a few stocks that are experiencing explosive gains or precipitous losses. To resolve this problem, we will be introduced to an adjusted price movement index (APMI) in a later chapter.

Summary:

In this chapter we have seen how it is possible use regression analysis to estimate one-month share-price gain and to compute regression residuals from the estimates of one-month share-price gain. It was suggested that these residuals provide powerful quantitative indication of the "outperforming" or "under-performing" condition of individual stocks. Stocks with high positive residuals are comparatively more likely to outperform in price gain over the next month. Conversely, stocks with high negative residuals are more likely to fall in price over the next month.

It was noted, however, that in order for these residual estimates to be useful, the correlation between one-month share-price gain and the price movement index (PMI) must be significant and meaningful. Also, it was pointed out that use of residual rankings instead of absolute residual estimates can help to overcome distortions introduced by changing market trends.

In the next chapter we will consider one final technical indicator, the relative strength index (RSI), and we will consider how it is possible to aggregate all of the technical indicators into one cumulative technical ranking index (CTR).

CHAPTER 6

THE RELATIVE STRENGTH INDEX (RSI) AND THE CUMULATIVE TECHNICAL RANKING INDEX (CTR)

> "Two are better than one, because they
> have a good reward for their labor."
> — ECCLESIASTES 4:9

The final technical indicator we will consider at this point in this book is the relative strength index (RSI). Relative strength is a way of comparing stocks in terms of their ratio of up days to down days over a specified period. The rationale is that stocks that are consistently closing each day at higher prices are to be preferred over stocks that are closing at lower prices or stocks that are flat with no price movement. The formula for the relative strength index (RSI) is as follows:

RSI = 100 − 100/ (1+y)

Where y = the average of X days of up closes divided by the average of X days of down closes. Typically the number of days in the specified period is set at 12 or 14, although other agreed periods can be used. Happily, there is no need for us to calculate the RSI for each stock each day because that information is routinely reported at websites such as *Finviz.Com* and *Stockcharts.Com*.

There remains some controversy over the interpretation of the RSI. The originator, Wilder (1978), proposed that an RSI value above

70 indicated that the stock or commodity was overbought and due for a downward correction, and an RSI value below 30 indicated that the stock or commodity was oversold and due for a rise in price. Many practitioners, such as *Finviz.Com*, follow Wilder's view that a high RSI (above 70) can be a portent of a likely decline in stock price. This interpretation suggests that there is a curvilinear relationship between RSI and future price direction. Other practitioners, such as *Investors' Business Daily* and this present author, single out those stocks with high RSI as potential buys. The fact that RSI shows a positive correlation with one-month price growth partially supports this latter view; although, an argument can be made that, if the RSI has been extremely high over a long period of time, there is no place for the stock price to go but down. Wisely, many technicians look for *divergences* as indicators of buying and selling opportunities. Thus for example, they focus on times when the RSI is rising above 70, but the share price has leveled or begun to decline, as an indication that it is time to sell. And they look for times when the RSI has been approaching 30, but the share price has leveled or begun to rise, as indications of buying opportunities.

Although RSI is a very useful indicator, it is not perfectly accurate. There are many examples of stocks with RSI values above 80 that have continued to rise in price for many days or weeks. Also, there are examples of stocks with RSI values below 30 that have continued to fall in share price. In addition, there is the vast middle ground where RSI values range between 30 and 70, and yet there are buying and selling opportunities there as well. In my own research efforts to identify the best buying opportunities for stocks, I have seldom if ever found a solid buying opportunity when the RSI was below 70, but that may be because I am a short-term trader and the methodology advocated here rewards higher RSI values in the ranking of stocks for purchase. Also, stocks making new highs in price tend to be those stocks with high RSI values.

Table 6.1 shows how the relative strength index (RSI) can be added to our spreadsheet and combined with the price movement index (PMI) and the cumulative momentum index (CMI) to derive a cumulative technical index (CTI).

GRANT HENNING PHD

TABLE 6.1. Twenty Stocks Arranged in Ascending Order of Cumulative Technical Ranking Index (CTR) on August 14, 2014.

A	P	N	S	T	U	V	W	X
Symbol	PMI	CMI	RSI	PMIr	CMIr	RSIr	CTI	CTR
PBYI	54.65	1015.84	83.04	1	1	8	10	1
RIC	17.44	223.16	83.69	14	15	7	36	2
BITA	13.03	548.33	88.56	31	5	1	37	3
ZEN	18.56	141.18	84.38	9	27	5	41	4
PLNR	18.44	191.10	79.00	10	19	16	45	5
PCRX	17.98	214.34	79.13	13	17	15	45	5
SLI	39.31	126.02	80.24	7	33	10	50	6
X	16.24	125.42	86.45	17	34	3	54	7
TSRA	20.29	86.78	84.29	5	50	6	61	8
HTCH	20.00	152.73	75.11	6	25	32	63	9
XRS	14.30	216.66	76.85	24	16	23	63	9
SPCB	23.65	226.55	71.18	2	14	50	66	10
CQB	18.38	68.03	86.62	11	57	2	70	11
PTRY	14.09	122.51	80.08	27	35	11	73	12
NVEC	17.19	50.06	77.29	15	67	22	104	13
FDO	15.27	68.44	74.35	19	56	34	109	14
SKX	14.21	131.47	70.75	26	31	53	110	15
TWOU	15.62	80.33	68.88	18	52	61	131	16
PTCT	7.45	154.73	68.81	54	24	62	140	17
SNSS	11.83	100.62	65.25	33	43	75	151	18

Note in Table 6.1 that once again certain columns have been dropped from the table in order that relevant information can be reported on a single page. Here we have twenty stocks arranged in ascending order of their cumulative technical rank (CTR) as of August 14, 2014. Of course, all of these rankings will have changed by the time you read this. Note also that this table adds columns S through X to our existing spreadsheet. In column S we have copied the RSI for each stock from the Finviz.Com website on the date noted. In columns T, U, and V, we have applied the Excel RANK function respectively to the PMI statistic from column P, to the CMI statistic from column N, and to the RSI statistic from column S. In this way we have derived the following ranking data: PMIr in column T, CMIr in column U, and RSIr in column V.

Because this is among the first of many applications of the Excel RANK function in this book, a little more explanation is warranted. The formula to be entered in cell T2 is as follows: =RANK(P2,$P$2:$P$95).

Once again, the dollar sign ($) signifies to Excel that the range for ranking is to be held constant throughout all rows of the iteration. The number 95 is given as the upper bound because there were 95 stocks in the database at that time. Once you have entered this formula in cell T2, you must then copy and drag it into all of the required cells in the T column. This will rank all of your stocks according to the magnitude of the price movement index (PMI), and so the T column is labeled (PMIr) accordingly.

The same procedure is followed to rank stocks according to the cumulative momentum index (CMI) in column U using the formula = RANK(N2,$N$2:$N$95) to be entered in cell U2 and copied and dragged down the U column. And again, the formula =RANK(S2,$S$2:$S$95) when entered into cell V2 and copied and dragged down that column, will rank all of your stocks according to relative strength.

The cumulative technical index (CTI) statistic reported in column W is simply the sum of the rankings reported in columns T, U, and V. Here the formula to be entered into cell W2 is as follows: =T2+U2+V2. This is then also to be copied and dragged down through all of the relevant rows in the W column. The smaller the value reported in column W, the better the stock is considered to be from an overall technical perspective. In a subsequent chapter we will revisit this statistic to show how it can be combined with fundamental data to promulgate a combined technical and fundamental ranking. The cumulative technical ranking statistic (CTR) in column X is just the ranking of the CTI using the same procedures.

Summary of Part One

So far in Chapters One through Five using our Excel spreadsheets we have derived several powerful technical indicators of the probability of near-term future share-price gain. Specifically, in column E we have calculated the multiple, which is the number of times the share price has multiplied from its low to the current price over the past 52 weeks. This is one indication of upward trajectory or annualized momentum.

In column F we have computed percentage lag, which is the proximity of current share price to 52-week high. In Chapter Two it was shown that use of percentage lag as an exclusive selection indicator led to four-month gains of 36 percent in a 20-stock portfolio. This was six times the gain of the S&P 500 Index during the same period. It was argued that percentage lag alone could serve as a profitable guide to equities trading, but that predictive efficacy could be enhanced still further through complementary use of other indicators provided in this book.

In Chapter Three we added columns I, J, and K, that represented respectively one-month, three-month, and cumulative one-plus-three-month percentage gain for the stocks in our database. It turns out that one-month percentage gain (or loss) is also a powerful indicator of positive (or negative) momentum that reflects likelihood of continuing gains (or losses). Three-month percentage gain is also useful as a comparative index and is needed for the subsequent computation of momentum and the Price Movement Index (PMI). It was suggested that the composite one-month-plus-three-month percentage gain index in column K could be used to remove stocks from our database when they cease to be of interest. Sorting from largest to smallest composite gain and removing all stocks with a value less than 40 in column K can serve this purpose.

Also in Chapter Three we added columns L, M, and N, that presented respectively one-month, 12-month, and cumulative momentum indices for stocks in our database. Concomitant research has concluded that momentum is possibly the strongest anomaly predicting future share-price gain (Zacks, 2011). Because of the ephemeral nature of momentum, we have provided both a short-term (one month) and a long-term (12-month) momentum index. For purposes of enhanced reliability of measurement, we have also included a cumulative momentum index (CMI) in column N.

In Chapter Four we have presented a unique price movement index (PMI). This was offered as a method of quantifying technical price movement patterns. In a subsequent chapter we will be introduced to an adjusted price movement index (APMI) that removes certain distortions inherent in the PMI.

In columns Q and R of Chapter Five we have seen how to compute one-month percentage-price-gain residuals for all of the stocks in our database. It was suggested that these residuals provide an important quantitative index of the degree to which individual stocks in our database are in either an "over-performing" or an "under-performing" condition. Stocks with positive residuals reflect over-performance and therefore represent comparatively better positive investments. Of all of the indicators in our spreadsheet thus far, this is clearly the most forward looking. It cannot be said that this one is a "lagging indicator" because it is a reflection of expected future price movement.

In Chapter Six we have explained and incorporated the relative strength index (RSI) in column S. We have also combined this index with the price movement index (PMI) and the cumulative momentum index (CMI) to form the cumulative technical rating (CTR) in column X. In subsequent analysis, I have found that stock *beta*s are also useful technical predictors that can also be built into the cumulative technical rating. But I did not discover this information in time to include it in the tables and formulas reported in this edition.

This concludes the basic work on technical indices in this book. Some technical traders may wish to stop here and make trading decisions based exclusively on technical indices. I myself frequently trade on the basis of the one-month momentum index in combination with a performance criterion that we will encounter in part three of this book. In the coming chapters we will look at fundamental ratios and find ways to integrate them and incorporate them into our system for the ranking of stocks. In the social sciences much of the process of combining variables relies on parametric statistics such as multiple regression analysis. I have already voiced my disenchantment with applying parametric statistics to stock market variables that fail to satisfy the requisite assumptions of normal and independent distribution. For this reason, throughout the remainder of this volume reliance will be placed primarily on nonparametric rank statistics and aggregate rank statistics.

PART TWO

FUNDAMENTALS

In this part of the book we will consider key fundamental indices and learn how to incorporate them into our system for the ranking of stocks. Requisite information for computing these indices is usually available from companies only on a quarterly basis. This is both good news and bad news for the trader. The good news is that it is not necessary to update fundamental data entries so frequently as it is in the case of technical data. But the bad news is that fundamental information is less current and less sensitive to real changes in companies than is technical information. Although technical information is usually more timely and sensitive, it is also more ephemeral than fundamental information. Ideally, both technical and fundamental information should be taken into consideration by the trader, so that when two stocks are found to have identical technical strength, preference should be given to the one with superior fundamentals. However, you may be shocked as I have been to see how very discrepant stock rankings may become depending on whether they are based on technical or fundamental information.

CHAPTER 7

CHOOSING FUNDAMENTAL INDICES

> "I made myself gardens and orchards, and I
> planted all kinds of fruit trees in them."
> — ECCLESIASTES 2:5

Equities fundamentals are usually expressed as ratios that imply underlying value in relation to price. Popular examples include price-to-earnings (PE) ratios, price-to-sales (PS) ratios, price-to-book (PB) ratios, return-on-equity (ROE) ratios, return-on-investment (ROI) ratios, return-on-asset (ROA) ratios, gross margins (GM), operating margins (OM), and profit margins (PM). Thus fundamental valuations are usually expressed as profitability statements, i.e., how much we must pay for a stock in relation to how much the company's performance suggests the stock is actually worth and is likely to return. Value traders are looking to find stocks that are undervalued in the marketplace and are therefore considered likely to provide a positive return on investment.

I had no idea at the outset how challenging this chapter would be to write. I have had to reanalyze data and rewrite this chapter several times because the outcomes have been so counterintuitive. On the surface, the task appeared simple at the beginning. All that was needed was to identify those fundamental indices that were most predictive of (i.e., most highly correlated with) one-month share-price growth, and find some way to aggregate those indices into a single powerful fundamental index. Accordingly, I used my database of the top 100 momentum stocks to study the correlations for 32 fundamental variables with one-month share-price percentage gain.

The fundamental variables studied included all of the following: book value per share, cash per share, analysts' mean recommendation (1-5), price-to-earnings (PE) ratio, forward price-to-earnings (FPE) ratio, price-to-sales (PS) ratio, price-to-book (PB) ratio, price-to-cash-per-share (PC) ratio, price-to-free-cash-flow (PFCF) ratio, quick ratio, current ratio, debt-to-equity (DE) ratio, long-term-debt-to-equity (LTDE) ratio, earnings per share (EPS), earnings-per-share estimate for next year, earnings-per-share estimate for next quarter, earnings-per-share growth this year, estimated earnings-per-share growth next year, annual earnings-per-share growth past five years, annual sales growth past five years, quarterly revenue growth year over year, quarterly earnings growth year over year, insider ownership percentage, institutional ownership percentage, return on assets, return on equity, return on investment, gross margin, operating margin, profit margin, ratio of shares outstanding to float, and analysts' mean target price. All of these were examined for their correlations with one-month price gain percentage.

And then came my first great shock. Contrary to expectation, the correlations of most of these major earnings variables with one-month share-price gain were actually negative. I spent weeks conjecturing about how this outcome could be possible. How could the systematic increase in earnings be positively related to share price decline? Surely I was doing something wrong. My first suspicion was that the problem was that I was focusing narrowly on one month share-price growth, whereas, earnings increases were usually reported quarterly. It follows that, if reported earnings are unchanged over a three-month period while share prices are increasing, this would create the appearance of a negative correlation between earnings and share-price gain when considered over a sufficiently large sample of stocks. For this reason, for fundamental variables, unlike my procedure with technical variables, I opted to use three-month share-price gain instead of one-month share-price gain as the dependent variable in order that sufficient time might be present for changes in reported earnings to take place.

My second great shock came when I found that those negative correlations between growth and earnings persisted—even after I broadened the time horizon from one to three months. Of the 32 fundamental variables studied, only five showed highly significant and meaningful correlations with three-month growth—all well above 0.50. However, all five of these variables showed correlations in the direction opposite to prediction. Specifically, the best predictive variables were price to sales (0.648), earnings per share (-0.542), annual sales growth over the past five years (-0.542), return on assets (-0.552), and profit margin (-0.531). Being a social scientist, I had no choice but to build these contrarian results into the subsequent model. I did, however, labor long in the attempt to find some explanation for these enigmatic results.

Ultimately I considered several possible explanations for these puzzling outcomes.

1. It is possible that my window of observation was still not broad enough. Had I observed share-price gain over a six-month or a twelve-month period instead of just a one-month or a three-month period, I may well have observed the desired positive correlations between earnings and growth. Unfortunately, however, my swing-trader style seldom permits me to hold stocks for such long periods. Furthermore, it has been my observation that very few stocks persist in share-price growth over long periods without periodic corrections. Therefore such long-term information is not useful to me, and it would fail to nullify the value of using the negative correlations over the shorter period of time that is the trading focus.
2. It is possible that we are witnessing the post-earnings-announcement-drift (PEAD) effect described by Zacks (2011). By this explanation, stocks rise in price at the initial announcement of positive earnings surprises, but then proceed to decline in price over succeeding weeks. This is a sort of "buy-on-the-rumor: sell-on-the-news" effect that could possibly account for the observation of a negative relationship between earnings and growth. As appealing as this explanation may seem, it fails to explain the pervasiveness of the correlational trends, because not all stocks report earnings at the same point in the quarter and not all earnings reported are in the same direction.

3. It is possible that the observed negative relationship between earnings and growth persists only for high momentum stocks. Because my sample of stocks for this study consisted entirely of high momentum stocks, it is possible that this resulted in a kind of sampling bias that predisposed the finding of a negative relationship between earnings and growth. Consistent with this explanation, on further investigation it has become evident that many of the stocks with the most rapid share-price gains are in the pharmaceutical and biotech sectors. Frequently such stocks have negative earnings and terrible fundamentals. This fact alone could certainly account for the negative correlations observed in this particular sample of stocks. Unfortunately, this outcome suggests that earnings may be positively related to growth in some sectors and negatively related to growth in other sectors. This weakens the case for the inclusion of fundamentals in any single model encompassing all sectors.
4. It may be that these negative correlational results represent a seasonal anomaly. It is possible that similar studies at other points in the market cycle would provide different results. It seems reasonable to conclude that a sudden sharp rise or decline in overall index averages could temporarily affect the correlations between those averages and reported earnings that have not yet changed. Although I have indeed observed some slight variations in the magnitudes of these correlations over time, the variations appear to be due more to the mix of stocks in the sample at any given time (e.g., the proportion of high growth biotech stocks present) than to overall market direction.

Although I currently favor explanation number three above, whatever the actual explanation may have been for these unanticipated outcomes, I decided initially to use the observed negative correlations in further modeling efforts. Not only did the fundamental side of my modeling initially employ a contrarian method of rewarding disappointing earnings, but you will see how this effect was compounded and intensified by the aggregation of the influence of all five fundamental variables mentioned above. This contrarian approach was initially successful whenever stocks such as those in the biotech sector were bullish and plentiful in my qualifying sample, but when the performance of such stocks turned bearish and were dropped from my sample several months later it became apparent immediately that it would be necessary to adjust polarity of fundamental rankings. That is part of the beauty of working within a spreadsheet system. One can always reverse the fundamental rankings with a single stroke and re-examine the outcomes. Currently I have reverted to using fundamental data exactly as it appears without any contrarian adjustment. I have found a need to compare the fundamental strengths of all equities, even if it turns out that fundamental data are less predictive of share-price gain than technical data are. In the end it turns out that earnings mean different things in different sectors of the market.

One very encouraging consideration has been found to serve as a compensating phenomenon for the contrarian results observed above. When you use residuals to rank stocks as shown in column R of Table 5.1, it turns out that the presumed advantages of negative fundamentals wash out. In other words, when you rank stocks from the highest positive residual to the lowest negative residual, those stocks with weakest fundamentals no longer tend to rise to the top as most desirable acquisitions. This observation, along with the observation of greater share price gains of stocks with positive residuals over stocks with negative fundamentals, has led me to give greater credence to residuals in future modeling efforts.

Table 7.1 below reports values for the five predictive fundamental variables price-to-sales ratio (PSR), earnings per share (EPS), five-year annual sales growth (5YSG), return on assets (ROA), and profit margin (PM) in columns S through W. These values have been added to an Excel spreadsheet with the top twenty stocks that were ranked from first to last for cumulative fundamental rank (CFR) as a subset of a database containing more than 70 stocks on July 31, 2014. Note that in those few instances where there were missing values, they have been accounted for by the insertion of the mean values for the respective columns. This is a standard procedure for attempting to eliminate bias in favor of any of the predictors. Where profit margins were not available, it was decided that return on assets provided the best approximation of profit margin.

Note also that columns W through AD employ the Excel RANK statistic as a means of ranking stocks on each variable and then to combine ranks. In the social sciences variables are often combined by using multivariate statistics such as stepwise multiple regression or principle components analysis. However, those approaches assume normal and independent distribution of data. Stock market data are neither normally nor independently distributed. For that reason and because the goal here is to rank stocks according to their relative prospective performance, it seemed appropriate in this case to aggregate variables by combining ranks. The precise procedure is described below for each variable appearing in Table 7.1.

TABLE 7.1. Five Fundamental Indices for 20 Stocks Arranged in Ascending Order of Cumulative Contrarian Fundamental Rank (CFR) on October 2, 2014.

A	Y	Z	AA	AB	AC	AD	AE	AF	AG	AH	AI	AJ
Symbol	PSR	EPS	5YSG	ROA	PM	PSRr	EPSr	5YSr	ROAr	PMr	CmFr	CFR
FOLD	430.48	-0.98	-51.6	-53.7	0	2	13	1	5	21	42	1
RCPT	361.73	-3.72	0	-61.1	0	3	2	16	3	21	45	2
TTPH	66.37	-2.21	0	-60.9	0	5	4	16	4	21	50	3
PIP	8.76	-0.21	-11.5	-65.4	-75.9	17	28	8	2	1	56	4
AGIO	76.9	-2.06	0	-28.3	0	4	6	16	14	21	61	5
RDUS	5	-29.84	0	-289.8	0	22	1	16	1	21	61	5
EXAS	751.99	-0.79	0	-35	0	1	14	16	12	21	64	7
TRUE	10.78	-0.53	0	-20.1	-21.6	15	19	16	16	4	70	8
OVAS	5	-1.87	0	-51.4	0	22	8	16	6	21	73	9
ESPR	5	-2.08	0	-42	0	22	5	16	9	21	73	9
BBLU	24.07	-0.58	0	-38.4	0	10	17	16	10	21	74	11
FLXN	5	-1.42	0	-43.5	0	22	12	16	8	21	79	12
MSON	5.06	-0.26	-18.5	-8.4	-9.2	21	26	4	22	7	80	13
MNDL	8.87	-0.54	4	-49.8	-70.7	16	18	37	7	2	80	13
IDSY	2.03	-0.64	-10.6	-13.8	-17.6	36	15	9	20	6	86	15
ZLTQ	6.41	-0.35	0	-14.9	-8.9	19	25	16	19	9	88	16
VRTX	30.05	-2.03	47.2	-20.5	-56.9	9	7	57	15	3	91	17
HTCH	0.47	-1.79	-16.9	-17.3	-19.6	56	9	6	17	5	93	18
RAIL	1.19	-1.55	-17.2	-4.8	-5.3	42	11	5	28	12	98	19
PTCT	32.28	-2.35	112.5	-30.3	0	8	3	59	13	21	104	20

Price-to-Sales Ratio (PSR)

As the name implies, the price-to-sales ratio (PSR) that is shown in column Y of Table 7.1 above reveals how much money in sales the company is experiencing in relation to the price of its shares. Because share price becomes the numerator of this ratio, the smaller the PSR is the better. A PSR of less than one is considered to be very healthy; whereas, a PSR over three begins to raise questions about the success of the company in moving its products. It follows that the PSR is a powerful indicator of the demand for the company's products and the company's marketing and distribution success. However, because Table 7.1 reports contrarian fundamental rank as discussed earlier in this chapter, in this case high PSR is rewarded with a higher equity ranking.

Most investors are more acquainted with the price-to-earnings (PE) ratio than they are with the PSR as an indicator of value. Unfortunately, it turns out that PE ratios are not very predictive of one-month or three-month growth according to my own research. This may be because earnings can legally be reported in many ways in order to make companies appear attractive at any given time. Another problem with the PE ratio is that, for stocks with negative earnings, no PE ratio is reported. And, since normally the smaller the PE ratio the better, it becomes confusing how to handle negative PE values. Over time the PE ratio may indeed represent value, and clearly that will be more the case for some companies than for other companies. For purposes of predicting share price growth however, I have found the price-to-sales ratio to be vastly superior to the price-to-earnings ratio. That is why use is made here of the former rather than the latter.

The current PSR for any publicly traded company can be found at many websites. However, an advantage in going to the Finviz.Com website is that all of the fundamental information of interest can be found on one page. Therefore, if you go there, you will want to enter the information required in columns Y through AC in Table 7.1 above simultaneously for each stock.

The next relevant task in preparation of our spreadsheet is to find the ranking of each stock in our database according to its PSR value. To do this we can use the Excel RANK statistic in column AD as shown above. The formula to be entered into cell AD2 is as follows: =RANK(Y2,$Y$2:$Y$70,0). Note that this formula says that we are returning to column Y that contains the PSR entries, and we are going to rank-order those entries beginning with cell Y2, and we will place the rankings into column AD. Use is made of the symbol $ because it is necessary to hold the range constant over which the ranking is to take place. The value 70 was entered because the database had exactly 70 rows on October 2, 2014. The number 0 is added at the end of the formula to tell the computer to arrange the stocks in order from the largest PSR value to the smallest PSR value. Remember that the smaller the PSR is the more sales the company is experiencing in relation to its share price, so to be consistent with our contrarian research findings we want the stocks with the largest PSR values at the top of our ranking in column AD. Once we have entered this formula into cell AD2, we must copy and drag it down through the rows for all 70 rows in our database. You will find that, as you drop stocks from your database, the value 70 will automatically correct to represent the new number of rows in your database. However, when you add new stocks to your database, you will need to change the number manually from 70 to the new value accordingly.

Earnings per Share (EPS)

The earnings-per-share (EPS) variable in column Z above is simply a statement of the amount of earnings in dollars over the past twelve months divided by the number of shares outstanding for a given company. The earnings-per-share variable is directly related to the price-earnings (PE) ratio. However, EPS has a profound advantage over the PE ratio for our purposes in that negative earnings are reported and represented in a scalable manner and there are not therefore so many instances of missing data.

The ranking formula for earnings per share (EPS) to be entered into cell AE2 on our spreadsheet should look like this: =RANK(Z2,$Z$2:$Z$70,1). Once again, this formula tells the computer to go to the Z column where the information is stored about earnings per share, and to rank those entries by magnitude from one to seventy. Again, the number 70 is based on the fact that our database had seventy rows at that time. The symbol $ is used to hold the range constant through all rows in the column. And the number 1 at the end of the formula tells the computer to begin the top of the column with the stock with the smallest earnings-per-share value. Recall that this contrarian arrangement was dictated by the research findings described at the beginning of this chapter. Once again it is then necessary to copy this formula from cell AE2 and paste it down the AE column.

Five-Year Annual Sales Growth (5YSG)

Five-year annual sales growth (5YSG) recorded in column AA of Table 7.1 is a measure of average annual sales growth expressed in percentages over the past five years. Presumably any company that is seeing a continuing escalation in sales of its products represents a good investment. Once again, however, research with our particular database supports a near-term contrarian interpretation of this fundamental variable. Another factor that may have contributed to the predictive power of this variable is the observation that many of the best momentum stocks have not yet been in existence for a total of five years. For those newcomers, a zero has been entered as a reflection of their lack of five-year annual sales growth. This means that, by our contrarian arrangement, a ranking advantage has inadvertently been given to new companies over companies that have been in existence for five or more years. That is what the numbers dictated, and that is what was therefore initially built into our model. Later on it has become apparent that zero is not always the best approximation for missing data. In Chapter 13 improved guidelines are presented for dealing with missing data.

The ranking formula for five-year annual sales growth (5YSG) that should be entered into cell AF2 is as follows: =RANK(AA2,$AA$2:$AA$70,1). After entry into cell AF2 this formula too should be copied and dragged down that column. Note that the interpretation of this formula is the same as the previous ranking formulas, thus the numeral one that appears at the end of the formula signifies that the stock with the smallest 5YSG value should appear at top of the column and be ranked as number one.

Return on Assets (ROA)

The return on assets (ROA) variable recorded in column AB of Table 7.1 indicates the percentage return over the past twelve months on total assets held by a company. Interestingly, although return on investment (ROI) and return on equity (ROE) also displayed significant correlations with three-month share price percentage growth in the same direction as ROA, the ROA correlation was of a higher magnitude and therefore it is the one included here.

The ranking formula for return on assets (ROA) to be inserted into cell AG2 is as follows: =RANK(AB2,$AB$2:$AB$70,1). Again, the value 70 was inserted because there were seventy stocks in this database at the time of data entry, but you will need to enter whatever value corresponds to the number of stocks in your spreadsheet database at the time of computation. Also again, the number 1 at the end of the formula tells the computer to arrange the stocks from lowest to highest on the variable of return on assets in accordance with our contrarian research findings. After entering this formula into cell AG2, once again you will need to copy and drag that entry down through all the rows of data in column AG.

Profit Margin (PM)

Profit margin recorded in column AC of Table 7.1 is the net profit margin for the trailing twelve months. This is net income as a percentage after all expenses have been deducted. We would expect this variable to be highly correlated with share-price gain, and it turns out to be one of the variables with the highest correlation. However, consistent again with our contrarian research findings, we need to enter stock rankings in reverse order for inclusion into our model.

The ranking formula for profit margin (PM) to be inserted into cell AH2 is as follows: =RANK(AC2,$AC$2:$AC$70,1). The interpretation of this formula is the same as was given for the previous fundamental variables entered in Table 7.1. Once again, after entering this formula into cell AH2, you will need to copy and drag that entry down through all the rows of data in column AH.

Combining Ranks

The process now gets interesting. We have a way to aggregate the fundamental data that does not require us to violate the assumptions underlying parametric statistics. We simply combine the rankings and rank the sums. We can see how this was done in columns AI and AJ of Table 7.1 above. To follow this procedure, first sum the fundamental variable rankings in columns AD through AH by entering the following formula into cell AI2: =AD2+AE2+AF2+AG2+AH2. Then copy and drag this formula down through all the occupied rows of the AI column. Finally, rank the sums that were entered into column AI by entering the following familiar formula into cell AJ2: =RANK(AI2,$AI$2:$AI$70,1). By now there is no need for me to interpret this formula for you. However, at this point it should be noted that, if the relationship between fundamental ranking and equity performance ceases to be contrarian due to cyclical market changes, this reversal can easily be accommodated by replacing the numeral one in the above formula with zero. As a matter of fact, at the time of this writing the fundamental relationships have righted themselves, so the formula to be entered into cell AJ2 is now as follows: =RANK(AI2,$AI$2:$AI$70,0). This formula will be further modified in that the number 70 will be changed regularly to correspond to the number of stocks in your database.

Amazingly, what we now have in column AJ is a ranking of all of the stocks in our database in accordance with what their most predictive fundamental characteristics suggest is the likelihood that their share prices will grow over the next three months! The aggregation of these fundamental variables in this manner serves to produce a Cumulative Fundamental Ranking (CFR) statistic that is more powerful than any of the individual fundamental variables taken in isolation. Bear in mind that this application was based on the contrarian correlations discussed at the beginning of this chapter, but has been altered to accommodate more current market conditions. Admittedly also this procedure does not allow for the individual weighting of variables to reflect their differential contribution to the overall explanation of variance in three-month share-price growth as might be accomplished through use of a multivariate statistical procedure such as stepwise multiple regression analysis. At the same time, we have not thereby unwittingly incorporated the powerful distortions that result from applying parametric statistics to non-parametric stock market data. From this comment you may properly conclude that this author is highly reluctant to apply certain multivariate parametric statistical procedures, such as multiple regression analysis, neural networking, and principal components analysis, to stock market data.

Summary

In this chapter we have seen how and why preference was given to five particular fundamental variables in the prediction of share-price growth. It was explained that three-month growth was employed as a dependent variable rather than one-month growth because earnings are usually reported on only a quarterly basis. It was further explained that, because the correlations of these variables with growth were negative, they were initially entered as contrarian predictors in our final model. It was noted that it subsequently became necessary to reverse polarity of fundamental rankings when market trends became more bearish.

It was shown how fundamental variable rankings could be combined to provide a final Cumulative Fundamental Ranking (CFR) of the stocks in our database. It was assumed that the composite of all fundamental variables would provide greater reliability of prediction than any one of those variables in isolation. Subsequently it has become apparent that positive fundamental data such as strong earnings may have a vastly different interpretation for stocks in different sectors of the market. Thus, strong earnings in the biotech and pharmaceutical sectors may be negatively correlated with growth, whereas it may be positively related to growth in many other sectors. This observation has led me to downplay the role of fundamentals in subsequent modeling efforts.

Now that we have taken a hard look at technical and fundamental ranking of stocks, it is time to see how we can derive composite rankings to provide more nearly global orderings of stocks to facilitate buying and selling decisions. Part Three of this book will address this task.

PART THREE

Composite Rankings of Stocks

In earlier chapters we have been introduced to a variety of technical and fundamental variables that serve as predictors of share-price growth. In this part of the book we want to see how those predictors may be combined to provide aggregate rankings of stocks for purposes of decision making about actual buying and selling.

CHAPTER 8

GLOBAL AGGREGATE RANKS

> "I also gathered for myself silver and gold and the
> special treasures of the kings and of the provinces."
> — ECCLESIASTES 2:8

Up to this point we have encountered a variety of technical and fundamental variables that may be used to predict one-month or three-month share-price gain in equities. You may have noticed that the rankings of stocks can be vastly different depending on which predictors are used at any given time. This discrepancy in rankings is nowhere more apparent than in technical *versus* fundamental rankings. For this reason it is useful to derive a global ranking of stocks that combines both technical and fundamental indicators. And it is also possible to harness the discrepancies between technical and fundamental rankings to make further share-price growth predictions. It turns out that stocks with highly discrepant technical and fundamental rankings tend to be more unstable than stocks with congruent technical and fundamental rankings. The discrepant stocks show a slight tendency to lose value, whereas the congruent stocks are more likely to gain in share price over the near term.

Deriving a Global Total Ranking Index

Table 8.1 shows how this Global Total Ranking (GTO) can be derived through use of the RANK statistic that we have encountered earlier. This table also reports an adjustment to the Price Movement Index (PMI) that was promised before. This was deemed necessary because it was found that the original PMI was too susceptible to outlier distortions. Also in Table 8.1 we can see how the discrepancy between technical and fundamental rankings can be used to derive a Technical-Fundamental Discrepancy Ranking (TFDr) to help in the prediction of future share-price direction.

TABLE 8.1. Twenty Stocks Arranged in Ascending Order of Global Total Ranking (GTO) of Combined Technical and Fundamental Indicators with Alternative PMI (APMI) and Technical-Fundamental Discrepancy Rankings (TFDr) As Noted on November 2, 2014.

A	B	X	AJ	AK	AL	AM	AN	AO
Symbol	Price	CTR	CFR	T+F	GTO	APMI	TFD	TFDr
RCPT	101.1	1	11	12	1	46.14	11	4
AGIO	83.75	3	14	17	2	52.38	13	5
RENT	80.45	13	6	19	3	22.23	10	2
ANAC	30.01	7	13	20	4	23.12	10	2
INFN	14.61	4	26	30	5	22.27	27	11
ESPR	29.34	15	16	31	6	26.56	7	1
IMDZ	29.55	29	4	33	7	4.66	32	13
MSON	13.85	32	2	34	8	6.71	38	15
RGLS	18.19	23	11	34	8	1.27	20	7
IG	9.93	16	22	38	10	42.64	16	6
STRP	20	38	5	43	11	6.71	44	20
VASC	29.39	9	36	45	12	25.44	39	16
TTPH	25.02	35	10	45	12	9.72	37	14
MACK	9.49	19	29	48	14	40.15	24	9
BBW	17.15	10	38	48	14	21.08	42	18
TRNX	27.94	18	31	49	16	13.93	29	12
ZLTQ	25.27	41	8	49	16	6	49	23
PTRY	26.09	12	39	51	18	20.47	45	22
LEAF	37.1	23	28	51	18	13.76	23	8
OVAS	20.49	5	49	54	20	29.03	64	34

As you can see in Table 8.1, it is now easily possible to combine our technical and fundamental rankings of stocks in order to derive a Global Total Ranking (GTO) as reported in column AL. Bear in mind that GTO can now become the single most focused overall indicator of equities desirability. It puts together into one index a composite of the best information available of both a technical and fundamental nature. Of course we will still want to consider other indices and several guidelines for timing of trades to be presented in subsequent chapters, but first let's consider the information available in Table 8.1.

Notice that the Composite Technical Ranking (CTR) from column X of Table 6.1 is here added together with the Composite Fundamental Ranking (CFR) from column AJ of Table 7.1 to produce a column of technical plus fundamental rank sums (T+F) in column AK. The sums in the AK column are then ranked by use of the RANK command, and the resulting rankings are entered into column AL in the same manner that we have seen previously.

The next matter of importance in Table 8.1 is the Alternative Price Movement Index (APMI) in column AM. As promised earlier, this column introduces a correction in the Price Movement Index (PMI) that was reported in column P of Table 4.1. It was subsequently discovered that that original PMI was sometimes too susceptible to distortions from outlier stock data. In order to correct that shortcoming, the following formula was entered into cell AM2 and dragged down the column for all stocks in the database: =P2+M2/10-F2*100. You can see from the columns P, M and F reported in Tables 1, 3, and 4 that this formula makes the Alternative Price Movement Index (APMI) to become a function of the original PMI, the 12-Month Momentum Index, and the Percentage Lag index. Hereafter, we should compare the correlation between one-month growth and the PMI with the correlation between one-month growth and the APMI. For purposes of computing residuals and all other applications of a price movement index should employ whichever variable, the PMI or the APMI, that exhibits highest correlation with one-month growth. This procedure should compensate for data outliers and seasonal distortions in the PMI. It should also ensure that the resultant correlation be significant and meaningful for purposes of applying the residual analysis.

Recently I have discovered yet another way to ensure that correlations be significant and meaningful for purposes of regression analysis. If you simply eliminate those stocks from your database that have the highest positive and negative residuals, the correlations on which the residuals are based will increase. Eliminating those stocks is analogous to saying that those stocks are outliers that do not fit the model. However, you, like me, may be unwilling to throw those stocks out because they may provide useful information in their own right. I am not willing to change the scope of reality in order to make my predictive models more powerful.

The Technical-Fundamental Discrepancy Index

One final piece of information is available in columns AN and AO of Table 8.1. There we have the Technical-Fundamental Discrepancy (TFD) Index and the TFD ranking (TFDr) column. If you have read my previous trading book, you will realize that I have long been curious about stocks that simultaneously have strong technical characteristics and weak fundamental characteristics, or conversely that have strong fundamentals accompanied by weak technical indicators. How can this happen? When it does (which is very often) what does it tell us about these stocks? Therefore, columns AN and AO have been added to provide experimental data to answer these questions. It turns out that there is some evidence that stocks which show the greatest discrepancies between their technical and fundamental rankings are also stocks that tend to decline in share price over the near term. To capture this phenomenon it is necessary to rank stocks according to their absolute discrepancies between final technical and fundamental indicators. Accordingly, in column AN we have the square root of the square (to remove minus signs) of the differences between the combined technical rankings (CTR from column X of Table 6.1) and the combined fundamental rankings (CFR from column AJ of Table 7.1). These absolute differences are then weighted by overall rank on the premise that the differences are less meaningful for stocks that are already highly ranked on most other criteria. The formula to be entered into cell AN2 and dragged down the AN column is as follows: =SQRT((AJ2-X2)*(AJ2-X2))+AL2.

The final step recorded in column AO of Table 8.1 is the ranking of stocks in accordance with their Technical-Fundamental Discrepancy (TFD) Index in column AN. The formula for this final step is as follows: =RANK(AN2,$AN$2:$AN$100,1). As we have seen previously, this formula is next inserted into cell AO2 and dragged down the AO column. Note that on November 2, 2014, the date of Table 8.1, my database had exactly 100 qualifying stocks and that is why the number 100 appears in this formula. Bear in mind again that the number of qualifying stocks in your database is subject to change after each day of trading, and it will be imperative to employ the same current total across all columns of your worksheet where the RANK statistic is being invoked.

Aggregation for Decision Making

Up to this point we have been introduced to a variety of criteria by which it is possible to rank stocks for purchase or sale. In fact, so much information has been presented in so few pages that your head may by now be swimming. You may be experiencing information overload. And yet it seems amazing to me that insights that have taken so many years to gather can be reduced to a few chapters in a book. The critical question you should now be asking is, "How can I best implement all of this information to make informed trading decisions?"

To answer this question let us return to the university admissions analogy. When students apply for admission to university, several admissions criteria must be satisfied. First of all they need to present acceptable standardized aptitude or achievement test scores to show that they can comprehend university-level instruction. They need to show a sufficiently high grade-point average or class ranking in high school to indicate that they have adequate study skills and a work ethic to achieve passing scores in a university classroom setting. They need letters of reference to attest to their character, perseverance, initiative, integrity, and likelihood to succeed. They may be asked to list memberships and leadership roles in organizations, societies, clubs, and sports to ensure that they possess socialization and leadership skills. They may be required to present a bank statement to show that they have sufficient finances to meet expenses. They may also need to write a letter of purpose to show that they can clearly articulate educational goals related to their targeted career pursuits. In addition they may at least at the graduate level be asked to participate in an interview to demonstrate requisite communication skills. Some military academies add to all of these requirements a letter of recommendation from a congressman and a medical examination report. Applicants are ranked according to each of these entry criteria, and only the top applicants are finally admitted. To my knowledge, the most stringent requirements of any university are those of the United States Coast Guard Academy that admits only the top six percent of all of its applicants—well beyond the standards of any ivy-league university.

Many other criteria could be added to the list of requirements, but because of the inevitable overlap in some of these criteria, little if any relevant new information is added after the first six or seven categories. Scientists have demonstrated through statistical techniques such as multiple regression analysis that little new variance in the dependent variable of academic achievement at university can be explained beyond what is provided by the six or seven best predictor variables. Beyond seven variables the law of diminishing returns comes into play, and many times there is little additional payoff beyond four or five predictor variables.

In years past I was fond of telling university graduate students that multiple indicators were necessary to establish measurement reliability. I would ask them how many character witnesses were needed to establish the good character of a prospective employee. The discussion would turn to matters such as how important the position was that was being filled, how well the character witnesses knew the person, how dependable the witnesses were, and whether or not there was general agreement among witnesses. But generally it was thought that the more witnesses found the better it would be, until it became too expensive or too time consuming to seek further witnesses. A similar problem occurs when an Olympic judging committee seeks to rate the performances of gymnasts, skaters, or divers. There needs to be a sufficient number of qualified judges to achieve reliable consensus. There needs to be an agreed upon rating schedule. There needs to be an agreed upon method of combining all of the ratings into a final score.

Deriving a Universal Index

Now let's consider this same process in the case of the selection of stocks for inclusion into a viable portfolio. Here too we should take advantage of a variety of predictor variables that may be viewed as meeting admission requirements. Like the admissions analogy example, some of these predictor variables will be related to past performance, some will be reflective of how well the stock is performing at present, and some will be more directly reflective of capacity for future performance. So far in this book we have encountered a number of viable predictor variables. Specifically, we have encountered the Global Total Ranking (GTO), Percentage Lag (%Lag), One-Month Percentage Gain (1MoGn), the Price Movement Index (PMI) or the Alternative Price Movement Index (APMI), One-Month Momentum (1MM), Growth-Estimation Residuals (Resid), the Relative Strength Index (RSI) and the Technical-Fundamental Discrepancy (TFD) Index. As we have seen repeatedly, it is now possible to rank the stocks in our database according to each of these predictor variables and combine these rankings to derive a Universal Index (UI) for purposes of decision-making about buying or selling.

In the case of predicting future stock performance, the problem is even thornier. Here we are combining rankings based on predictors that take into consideration patterns of both technical and fundamental information suggesting that the price of a stock is likely to increase. These technical and fundamental indicators often may not agree. Furthermore, we are combining these rankings with other information such as residual rankings that suggest how far stock price increases may have overshot or undershot predictions and may therefore regress to a mean estimate. In short, we are combining multiple unidimensional indicators to form a single scale of future stock performance that is likely a multidimensional phenomenon. In terms of measurement theory, we are trying to define a single multidimensional "latent trait" of future stock performance through use of our multiple unidimensional indicators. Although in this effort we are destined or doomed to a certain amount of inaccuracy, we can be content as long as our predictions serve to improve decision-making. This process is like the measurement of human weight where we do not need to be accurate to the milligram as long as we can know the extent to which the person to be measured is overweight or underweight for practical purposes by comparison with others.

Table 8.2 indicates how our multiple indicators can be combined into a single Universal Index (UI) for decision-making purposes.

GRANT HENNING PHD

TABLE 8.2. Twenty Stocks Arranged in Descending Order of Universal Index (UI) Ranking in a Database of 98 Stocks on November 21, 2014.

A	R	AP	AQ	AR	AS	AT	AU	AV	AW	AX	AY	AZ	BA
Symb	Res	Rr	MG	1MM	GR	%Lag	1MG	APM	1MM	Res	RSI	TFD	UI
RDCM	40.24	95	2	2	1	1	1	1	1	1	-1	1	1	6
PAYC	20.16	85	4	4	1	1	1	1	1	1	-1	1	1	6
MRGE	-12.4	3	16	6	1	1	0	1	1	1	1	-1	0	4
AMOT	-5.73	17	13	5	0	1	1	1	1	1	0	1	-1	4
ODP	-3.85	23	33	10	1	1	0	1	1	1	0	-1	1	4
INCY	0.31	40	22	7	1	1	0	0	1	1	0	0	1	4
RDI	-4.84	20	37	14	0	1	0	0	1	1	0	1	0	3
RCPT	43.47	96	3	3	1	0	1	1	1	1	-1	-1	1	3
CTP	-3.67	25	12	11	1	0	1	1	1	1	0	-1	0	3
RIC	-8.89	10	54	42	1	0	-1	1	-1	1	1	0	1	2
ANIP	45.98	97	1	1	0	0	1	1	1	1	-1	1	-1	2
OVAS	26.96	92	7	13	1	-1	1	1	1	1	-1	0	0	2
YHOO	-1.86	30	38	19	0	1	0	0	0	0	0	1	0	2
ABMD	6.87	62	15	8	0	0	0	0	1	1	-1	1	0	1
AGIO	15.3	77	20	35	1	0	0	1	0	0	-1	-1	1	1
NXTM	-7.57	12	69	52	0	0	-1	0	-1	-1	1	1	1	1
ZLTQ	-3.18	26	61	36	1	0	-1	0	0	0	0	-1	1	0
SWIR	9.08	67	18	27	1	-1	0	-1	0	0	-1	1	1	0
MIK	0.76	42	53	17	0	1	-1	0	0	0	-1	1	-1	-1
KONA	7.93	64	21	16	0	0	0	-1	0	-1	-1	0	1	-1

You will notice in Table 8.2 that once again certain columns have been dropped from our spreadsheet to allow space to present the table on a single page. You will notice also that on November 18, 2014, this database contained exactly 98 stocks in accordance with our rules for adding and deleting stocks from the database. Columns A and R are self-explanatory in that they simply report the stock symbols from column A of our spreadsheet and the residual values from column R of our spreadsheet. In column AP we are shown the rankings of stocks according to the residual values in column R. Next, in column AQ we are given the rankings of stocks according to one-month percentage gain as given in column I of our spreadsheet. And then in column AR we are presented with the rankings of stocks in accordance with one-month momentum as shown in column L of our spreadsheet. These three columns (AP, AQ, and AR) employ the RANK function as we have seen before and use the following three formulas respectively: 1. =RANK(R2,$R$2:$R$98,1)

2. =RANK(I2,$I$2:$I$98,0) and 3. =RANK(L2,$L$2:$L$98,0). Note that the primary distinction among these three formulas is that the first formula for ranking residuals gives first ranking to stocks with lowest residuals; whereas, the second and third formulas give first ranking to stocks with highest one-month percentage gain and highest one-month momentum respectively, as indicated by the numerals 1 or 0 at the end of each formula.

We are now ready to understand how the Universal Index (UI) in column BA at the far right side of Table 8.2 is derived. It simply reports the sums of the scores awarded to each stock in columns AS through AZ. Those scores may be 1, 0, or -1, depending on how the stock is ranked by each of the predictor variables concerned. Thus, in column AS we have the scores awarded to each stock depending on whether it ranks in the top 14 (+1), from 15 through 39 (0), or 40 or above (-1) on the variable of Global Total Ranking (GTO). The formula used to award the scores is as follows: =IF(AL2<15,1,IF(AL2>40,-1,0)). Accordingly, this formula is inserted in cell AS2 and dragged down the AS column.

In column AT, scores are awarded to each stock on the basis of how far in percentage terms its price now lags below its 52-week high. By this process a zero-to-two percentage-point lag is awarded one point. A two-to-five percentage-point lag is awarded zero points. And finally, anything beyond a five percentage-point lag is awarded a minus one point. The formula in this case is as follows: =IF(F2<0.02,1,IF(F2>0.05,-1,0)). Here again this formula is inserted into cell AT2 and dragged down the AT column.

In column AU, points are awarded to each stock in accordance with percentage gain in share price over the past month. Because of market vicissitudes, it is better to award points on the basis of comparative ranking than on the basis of absolute percentage gain. For this reason the formula used in column AU is as follows: =IF(I2<15,1,IF(I2>40,-1,0)). Notice that, as was the case with Global Total Ranking in column AS, the top fourteen stocks are each awarded one point. Stocks ranking fifteenth through fortieth on monthly percentage gain are awarded zero points. Stocks ranking above forty are each awarded a minus one point. This formula is then inserted into cell AU2 and dragged down the column.

Column AV reports the scores awarded for price movement ranking or alternative price movement ranking. Recall that the Price Movement Index (PMI) in column P of our spreadsheet and its ranking in column T of our spreadsheet is the variable of interest here. However, in rare situations when market conditions dictate that our PMI ceases to have a significant and meaningful correlation with one-month percentage gain, we look for an Alternative Price Movement Index (APMI) such as the one presented in column AM of our spreadsheet. It turns out that such a situation is a rare occurrence so that there is no need to belabor this point. At the time of this writing, the Price Movement Index is serving our purpose very well and there is no need to look for an alternative, so that the formula used in column AV is as follows: =IF(T2<15,1,IF(T2>40,-1,0)). This formula is inserted into cell AV2 and dragged down the column.

Column AW shows points awarded for one-month momentum. The source for this ranking is found in column AR. Thus, the formula to be entered into cell AW2 and dragged down the AW column is as follows: =IF(AR2<15,1,IF(AR2>40,-1,0)). It was determined that the one-month momentum index is more sensitive to momentum changes than other momentum indexes we have encountered.

Column AX reports scores awarded for residual ranking as that ranking has been recorded in column AP. As noted earlier, this is an indication of the extent to which stocks may be in an overbought or oversold condition and it serves as a check on stocks that may have run up in price too quickly. Here the formula to be entered into cell AX2 and dragged down the AX column is as follows: =IF(AP2<15,1,IF(AP2>40,-1,0)).

Column AY lists the scores awarded for relative strength ranking as was given in column V of our spreadsheet. Recall that relative strength (RSI) recorded in column S of our spreadsheet should be updated at the end of trading each day. The formula to be entered into cell AY2 and dragged down the AY column is as follows: =IF(V2<15,1,IF(V2>40,-1,0)).

The final component that was entered into Table 8.2 for the promulgation of our Universal Index (UI) is found in column AZ. There we have scores awarded for technical-fundamental discrepancy. You will remember that it was discovered that stocks which displayed greatest discrepancy between technical and fundamental ranking were also stocks that tended to decline in price. The Technical-Fundamental Discrepancy ranking is available in column AO of our spreadsheet. Therefore the formula for awarding scores for this discrepancy ranking is as follows: =IF(AO2<15,1,IF(AO2>40,-1,0)). This formula is then entered into cell AZ2 and dragged down the AZ column.

The final column BA on the right-hand side of Table 8.2 reports the Universal Index (UI) for the stocks in our database. As you can see, the Universal Index is simply the sum of the scores for each stock on the eight predictor variables for which we have rankings. Therefore this index can range in magnitude from +8 to -8. The higher the positive sum may be, the more desirable the stock will be for acquisition. The formula to be entered into cell BA2 and dragged down the BA column is as follows: =AS2+AT2+AU2+AV2+AW2+AX2+AY2+AZ2. You will recognize that it will be easy enough to drop variables from or add variables to the Universal Index by simply modifying this formula should it ever become desirable to do so.

For the record, it is now several months since I first developed the Universal Index comprised of the seven components listed in Table 8.2. I have already made a few modifications to strengthen the index that have not been discussed elsewhere in this book. Some of the initial components have been replaced and the total number of components has grown from seven to ten. To make these changes it was necessary to test each prospective component of the index for predictive efficacy. An innovative way to test each prospective component was to mark the symbols of all stocks exceeding daily gains of two percent. Next, it was possible to sort the stocks according to each predictive variable in the spreadsheet and to count the numbers of stocks exceeding two percent gains that were in the top fifteen ranking by each predictive variable. Currently the surviving Universal Index components are as follows: Combined Technical Ranking (replacing GR as being a better predictor of gain), Percentage Lag (%Lag), One-Month Percentage Gain (1MG), Momentum/Adjusted Price Movement Ratio (replacing APM as being a better predictor of gain), One-Month Momentum Ranking (1MM), Positive Residual Ranking (Res), Multiplication off 52-Week Lows (Mult—replacing RSI as being a better predictor of gain), Technical-Fundamental Differentiation (TFD), 52-Week Multiplication/

Percentage Lag Ratio (added to improve predictive accuracy), Beta (added to improve predictive accuracy).

Summary:

In this chapter we have seen how it is possible to aggregate information from a variety of technical and fundamental indicators to provide global indicators for decisions regarding which stocks are desirable to buy or sell for purposes of maintaining our own personal portfolio of stocks. In this way a Universal Index (UI) has been promulgated as the best composite indicator of equity acquisition desirability. It has also been shown how this index can easily be modified over time to incorporate only those components that are most predictive of share-price gain.

To this point we have been exposed to a variety of technical, fundamental, and global indicators of the desirability of particular equities. In the next section of the book we shall observe different strategies for implementation of this information. By analogy, if we have so far amassed a great arsenal, in the next chapter we shall see how it may be most appropriate to use this arsenal to enter into battle.

PART FOUR

Trading Strategies

In previous chapters we have learned how to rank stocks according to a variety of technical, fundamental, and aggregate indicators. In this next section we will consider a variety of trading strategies that make use of the information we have accumulated so far. For those with eyes to see, this transition to implementation will present a kaleidoscopic concatenation of boundless splendor. It is like descending into an underground cavern with symmetrical fluorescent crystalline displays of breathtaking beauty. It is this same sense of awe and wonder that makes the daily drudgery of data entry seem easily endurable. Chapter Nine will present momentum strategies, including the percentage lag strategy that was mentioned briefly in Chapter Two. Chapter Ten will present performance strategies that are based on information about the comparative performance of stocks in the database.

CHAPTER 9

IMPLEMENTING MOMENTUM TRADING STRATEGIES

> "So I perceived that nothing is better than that a man should rejoice in his own works, for that is his heritage. For who can bring him to see what will happen after him?"
> — ECCLESIASTES 3:22

Our purpose in this chapter is to show how the information we have gathered about equities momentum in previous chapters may be employed in actual trading strategies. In particular, we will look at the percentage lag strategy first discussed in Chapter Two and then we will explore four other momentum strategies. There has been no effort to present these strategies in any preferential order. In fact, any one of the strategies presented may become most suitable at different seasons and under different market conditions. Also, trading in some ways resembles hazardous rock climbing in the way that three appendages of the body are recommended to be attached to the rock at any time. Similarly, it is useful in point of safety always to have your eyes on several different indicators at any given time. Thus, you will see a theme repeated throughout this section whereby focus is made on a primary indicator with confirmation sought by using at least two additional indicators.

Before we begin to look at strategies however, there are several housekeeping procedures that you will find helpful. First, now that we have developed a very wide spreadsheet consisting of 53 columns in all, you will find it beneficial to copy column A with the stock symbols somewhere onto each page of your spreadsheet so that it will not be necessary to scroll back to the far left of the spreadsheet to recognize the stocks considered on each page. Happily, this will not adversely affect the formulas embedded in the spreadsheet because Excel automatically adjusts those formulas to reflect column changes. Alternatively, Excel has a procedure that allows you to hold the first column on the same page as you scroll through successive pages. Eventually you may also wish to copy onto the first page of your spreadsheet those columns that you wish to use for decision-making purposes. That way you can immediately view the changes in your decision making vectors with any intraday changes in stock prices without the need to scroll through the entire spreadsheet. However, for easy reference purposes in this book I will continue to refer to the variables in our spreadsheet as occupying the columns with the same letter headings displayed in the earlier tables of this book, extending from column A to column BA. And any new columns required in the future will follow immediately after column BA.

1. The Percentage Lag Strategy

As was demonstrated in Chapter Two, "percentage lag" or "proximity to new 52-week highs" as shown in column F of your spreadsheet is itself one of the most powerful indicators of the desirability of acquiring and holding or selling stocks in your database. Earlier I explained that all good stocks may be expected to reach new highs in price, and it is often as they approach or surpass those new highs that the stocks become most attractive to the investment community. I used the analogy of a waterfall by claiming that stocks usually gain trading volume as they approach new highs just as a river accelerates as it approaches a waterfall. For this reason a percentage-lag strategy may also be viewed as one kind of momentum strategy. It is perhaps the simplest momentum strategy to implement.

    a) The first step in implementation is to return to column F of your spreadsheet where percentage lag is recorded for all stocks in your database. Sort this column from the smallest to the largest value so that stocks closest to new highs appear at the top.

b) Next focus on the top twenty stocks in the column. Depending on market conditions, these will all be within 1.5 percent of the 52-week highs. These become the initial candidates for acquisition.
c) As a next step you should look for ancillary confirmation. Here you are narrowing the list of candidates by considering other indicators of interest. One helpful indicator at this point is the number of times the stock price has multiplied above its 52-week low. This is the Mult variable listed in column E. By choosing stocks with Mult values above 2.2 you should be able reduce the number of qualifying stocks to less than five.
d) As a final selection step you might go to column BA to select from among the remaining candidates the stocks with the highest Universal Index (UI) values.

By this strategy you will never purchase a stock that is more than 1.5 percent below its 52-week high. For decisions about selling a stock you can use the strategy in reverse. You can employ a rule to sell all stocks whose prices fall below three percentage points off their 52-week highs unless they continue to be in the top ten by Multiple (Mult) ranking and Universal Index (UI) ranking. However, barring extenuating circumstances, all stocks declining below four percent below their 52-week highs should be sold. This particular strategy has the strength that losers will be quickly culled out of any portfolio and winners will be maintained.

It will be obvious to you that this strategy has many possible variations depending on the ancillary variables you choose and depending on the cut-off scores you select. There are so many possible nuances to this strategy that it may even be said that percentage lag strategy represents an entire family of possible strategies to choose from.

2. The One-Month Momentum Strategy

In the implementation of this strategy primary use is made of the information on one-month momentum (1MM) that is found in column L of your spreadsheet. Experience has shown that 12-month momentum as reported in column M of your spreadsheet is not sufficiently sensitive to current directional trends to warrant use in swing trading. One-month momentum by contrast tends to be overly sensitive, with wild intraday changes in rankings. One solution to this problem is to combine one-month momentum (1MM) scores with the alternative price movement index (APMI) found in column AM of your spreadsheet. This results in a patterned one-month momentum index (POMI) that is both more stable and more reflective of price movement patterns over the past three months.

a) The first step of implementation is to create the patterned one-month index (POMI) in a new column (BB at the far right side of your spreadsheet). The formula for this new index is as follows: =L2+AM2. This formula is inserted into cell BB2 and dragged down the BB column which is then labeled POMI in cell BB1. As you can see, this formula combines one-month momentum (1MM) with the alternative price movement index (APMI) to produce a stable momentum indicator.

b) Next sort the BB column from largest to smallest so that the largest POMI values are at the top of the column.

c) Focus only on the top stocks in the column with POMI values above 50. These become the critical stocks from your database for possible acquisition. Depending on market conditions, this should reduce the scope of inquiry to less than 20 stocks.

d) For further reduction in the scope of inquiry, seek ancillary confirmation with other indicators in your spreadsheet. For example, you may now go to column BA and inspect the Universal Index (UI) for all stocks. By selecting only those remaining stocks with UI values at five or above, you can reduce the number of qualifying stocks to only two or three, depending on market conditions.

e) As a final delimiter, you may go to column AP and choose the remaining stock with the highest residual ranking. Hopefully this will identify a stock with a residual ranking greater than 50. This should maximize the chances that the stock is superior in performance. At any given time it is possible to verify the efficacy of the residual ranking by correlating it with percentage lag. The correlation should be positive, significant, and meaningful.

Inasmuch as both of the strategies described so far are momentum strategies, it is possible that the same stocks will be identified for purchase by either strategy. A variety of ancillary predictors may be used to make final decisions about purchase or sale of stocks. For example, one may choose to employ the same percentage lag strategy for determining the exit point with any other strategy and thus determine to sell stocks when their prices drop more than four percentage points below their 52-week highs. The exact choice of procedure may be dictated by market conditions, by experience, or merely by trader temperament.

3. The Cumulative Momentum Strategy

Because, as was noted with the implementation of the previous strategy, one-month momentum is often too sensitive and subject to intraday swings, and twelve-month momentum is often too insensitive and intransigent, another way to overcome these problems is to use the Cumulative Momentum Index of column N as your starting point. Cumulative momentum combines one-month with twelve-month momentum and this provides a more stable and reliable momentum indication. Because of its partial reliance on twelve-month momentum, this strategy incorporates a broader time window within which to operate.

a) Begin this strategy by going to column N of your spreadsheet and sorting from largest to smallest on cumulative momentum.
b) Focus attention on the top stocks with cumulative momentum values above 100. This should reduce the scope of inquiry to 20 stocks or less.
c) As the next step choose another ancillary indicator to reduce the candidate stocks still further. For example, you may choose the Price Movement Index (PMI) of column P. Find the two or three candidate stocks with the highest PMI values.
d) As a final confirmatory step, go to yet another ancillary indicator for final selection. Here, by way of example, you may choose the

remaining stock with the lowest Global Total Ranking (GTO) value in column AL, or you may choose the stock with the smallest percentage lag in column F.

Once again, decisions about selling may be made with reference to the percentage lag values in column F. Any stock with a greater than four percentage-point departure from its 52-week high may be considered a candidate for sale unless extenuating circumstances exist.

4. The Multiple Ratio Momentum Strategy

A final momentum strategy discussed in this book makes use of the Multiple (Mult) index of column E of your spreadsheet, that was discussed in Chapter One. Recall that this column reports the number of times the stock price has multiplied from its low over the past 52 weeks. As such, the column represents the long-term upward trajectory of the stock. To promulgate the Multiple Ratio Index (MRI) used for this strategy, it is necessary simply to divide this value by percentage lag using the following formula: =E2/F2.

- a) As step one of this strategy, the MRI formula above is inserted into cell BC2 of your spreadsheet and is copied and dragged down the BC column. This new column should be labeled MRI in cell BC1.
- b) Sort this column from largest to smallest with the largest values at the top.
- c) Focus on the top twenty stocks in the column. All of them should have MRI values in excess of 100.
- d) Seek ancillary confirmation by consulting another indicator. For example, one might look for remaining stocks in column AS with a Global Total Ranking (GTO) less than ten. This should restrict the number of qualifying stocks to less than five.
- e) Finally, as a last step find the stock with the highest residual ranking in column AP, or the highest Universal Index (UI) ranking in column BA.

Interestingly, the MRI index is among the most volatile of the momentum indices. Because it employs percentage lag as a divisor, MRI values can vary wildly intraday. This allows the index to be highly sensitive to intraday momentum, and this sensitivity can be extremely valuable in its own right. At the same time this volatility underscores the importance of using ancillary confirmation in the decision-making process.

5. The Patterned Price Movement Strategy

One of the most innovative of the technical indicators produced in our spreadsheet so far is the Price Movement Index (PMI) found in column P of the spreadsheet. Provided that all of your data entry is current—including daily, one-month, and three-month stock prices—the PMI supplies a quantitative reflection of propitious charting patterns of the stocks in your database.

a) First, go to the Price Movement Index in column P of the spreadsheet and sort the column from largest to smallest values, so that the stocks with largest PMI values appear at the top of the column. Limit your focus to the top 15 stocks in the column.

b) Next, go to the Universal Index (UI) in column BA of your spreadsheet. Choose those stocks with UI values of five or above. This should reduce the number of stocks of interest to fewer than five, depending on market conditions.

c) Finally, inspect the Multiple Ratio Index (MRI) in column BC to find the remaining stock(s) with highest momentum values.

Remember that, as a rule, any stock with a percentage lag value above 0.04 is a candidate for sale unless extenuating circumstances dictate that the stock be held longer.

Summary:

In this chapter we have observed five proposed momentum trading strategies that rely on information previously generated in your spreadsheet.

Specifically, we have considered the Percentage Lag Strategy, the One-Month Momentum Strategy, the Cumulative Momentum Strategy, the Multiple Ratio Momentum Strategy, and the Patterned Price Movement Strategy. Each of these strategies requires the use of additional indicators to provide ancillary confirmation for the identification of preferred alternative stocks. Although any one of the strategies may be found more appropriate under different market conditions, it goes without saying that, if the same stocks are identified as winners by more than one of these strategies, this will lend even greater confidence to your decision to buy. Ideally, in times when market conditions are extremely adverse, there will be no stocks qualifying for acquisition or maintenance in your portfolio by any of these strategies.

CHAPTER 10

Implementing Performance Trading Strategies

Although research has suggested that momentum is quite possibly the most important anomaly predictive of upward or downward price movement, there are other effective predictors of price movement as well. In this chapter we shall examine a cluster of strategies related to what we may call "performance." In this context "performance" refers to how a stock has behaved with respect to a variety of criteria. Performance strategies favor stocks that have performed well up to the present time. The rationale here is that stocks which have consistently performed well up to the present time are likely to continue to perform well on average in the near future.

1. The One-Month Gain Strategy

This strategy gives primary attention to comparative gains that stocks have made over the past month. You will notice that the spreadsheet as constructed in Chapter Three employs columns I, J, and K for one-month, three-month, and one-month-plus-three-month percentage gains respectively. For purposes of trading stocks, the one-month column is the most useful because it reflects the most recent equity performance.

    a) As the first step in implementing this strategy you should go to column I and sort the stocks from largest to smallest gains, with those stocks having largest one-month percentage gains at the top of the column. You will need to focus on the top 20 stocks in the column.

b) Because one-month percentage gains are highly volatile at the upper end, it is important next to seek ancillary support. A good variable to consider next for this purpose is the Universal Index (UI) in column BA that was presented in Chapter Eight. This is a global performance indicator that registers performance across multiple dimensions. Now you can restrict your search further to those stocks with UI values of five or above. This should confine your search to fewer than five stocks, depending on market conditions.

c) As a final step in stock selection, go to the Percentage Lag (%Lag) column F reported in Table 1.1 and choose the remaining stock(s) that are in closest proximity to the fifty-two week high(s). Here again the rationale is that stocks with share prices far from the fifty-two week highs are subject to the problem of overhang and are less likely to move upward in price to new highs as quickly as stocks with no overhang.

2. The Universal Index Strategy

The Universal Index (UI) described in Chapter Eight is a composite of eight different performance measures. Depending on relative position on each of those composite measures, the Universal Index value for any given stock may range from minus eight (-8) to plus eight (+8). Because of the broad reflection of performance provided by the Universal Index, it is an excellent place to begin a performance strategy. Bear in mind that stocks with negative UI values are not necessarily bad investments over the long term and therefore this index should not be used to pick stocks for shorting.

a) Begin implementation of this strategy by going to column BA of your spreadsheet where the Universal Index (UI) is located. Sort the column from largest to smallest so that stocks with the largest UI values are located at the top of the column.

b) Focus mainly on those stocks with UI values of five or above if possible. This should restrict your search to fewer than ten stocks, depending on market conditions. In times when no

stocks qualify, it is likely that market conditions are such that you should take no long positions in stocks.
c) Next, for ancillary support go to column AP and restrict your search still further to those stocks that have the highest residual ranking based on their performance.
d) Finally, go again to the Percentage Lag column F and choose the stock(s) that are in closest proximity to their 52-week highs. As you can see, percentage lag is often the final honest broker of stock performance.

3. The Global Total Performance Strategy

Another key performance indicator that we have encountered earlier is the Global Total Ranking (GR) that appears in column AS of your spreadsheet. Recall that this indicator is a macro combination of five technical indicators (i.e., percentage lag, one-month percentage gain, the price movement index, total momentum, and relative strength) and five fundamental indicators (i.e., the price-to-sales ratio, the earnings-per-share ratio, five-year sales percentage, return on assets, and profit margin), with overall technical and fundamental factors weighted equally. It is important to remember that the fundamental component of this performance indicator was initially contrarian in nature, but it became reversed when later market conditions reflected a positive relationship between equities fundamentals and near-term growth. You can see the Global Total Ranking (GTO) used in this strategy and the Universal Index (UI) involved in the previous strategy are the two most comprehensive performance indicators presented so far in this book.

a) As the first step in implementing this strategy, go to the Global Total Ranking (GR) reported in column AS of your spreadsheet and sort the column from smallest to largest so that the preferred stocks appear at the top of the column.
b) Focus exclusively on the top fifteen stocks in the column.
c) Next look for ancillary confirmation by observing the ranking scores of the Universal Index column BA of your spreadsheet. Here again you should restrict your search to stocks with a UI

value of five or above. This should reduce your search to fewer than five stocks. If no stocks qualify, that is likely an indication that market conditions are not suitable for acquiring long positions in your equities portfolio.

d) As a final step to pick the most promising stock(s) by this strategy, go next to the percentage lag column F and choose the remaining stock(s) with the smallest value, preferably less than 0.02 and/or go the Multiple Ratio Index column and choose the stock(s) with the highest momentum value.

4. The Comprehensive Performance Strategy

This strategy seeks to take advantage of two of the most comprehensive indicators of performance in our spreadsheet in order to compile the single most comprehensive indicator of performance in our repertoire, the Comprehensive Performance Index (CPI), to be placed in column BD of our spreadsheet. The two indicators that form the starting point of this strategy are the Grand Total Ranking (GTO) in column AL and the Universal Index (UI) in column BA. The formula then for the computation of the CPI is as follows: =10*SQRT(AL2)/(BA2+9). This formula is placed in cell BD2 and dragged down the BD column.

a) As a first step after you have applied the formula above, go to the Comprehensive Performance Index (CPI) in column BD of your spreadsheet.

b) Sort the values in the column from smallest to largest with the smallest values at the top of the column. Focus attention on the top 15 stocks in the column.

c) For ancillary confirmation go to the Universal Index (UI) column BA and pick those stocks with a UI value of five or above. This should limit your search to around five or fewer stocks, depending on market conditions.

d) Finally, to take advantage of forward trending information go to the residual ranking information in column AP and choose the stock(s) with the highest ranking numbers, preferably above 60. This will serve to identify the outperforming stock(s) in the list.

As always, it is good to consider the possibility of selling those stocks with percentage lag above four percent.

5. The Future Trend Strategy

Up to this point our performance strategies have been partially based on the assumption that past performance is a valid portent of future performance. Although that assumption may be warranted as an overall statistical average, there are some cases where it does not fit. It may be safe to assume that, because the sun has appeared to rise in temperate zones every morning throughout recorded history we can expect to see some daylight tomorrow morning. It may not be safe to assume that, because the price of a certain stock has risen every week in the past quarter, it will rise next week—even if statistical odds are in favor of its rising. In fact, it sometimes happens that stock prices become inflated in such a way that the most productive stocks are ripest for a downward correction. Stocks that show the most rapid ascent in price often also show the most rapid descent.

In order to employ this strategy, it will be necessary first to compute a Future Trend Index (FTI). To do this we must take advantage of residual analysis that we first encountered in Chapter Five. If we combine the Residual Ranking (Rr) with the Universal Index Ranking (UIr) we can derive an estimate that combines what is likely to happen with what has already happened. The FTI then seeks to combine the future with the past. We already have computed the Residual Ranking (Rr) in column AP of our spreadsheet. It remains to transform the Universal Index (UI) of column BA into a Universal Index Ranking (UIr) and insert it into column BE of our spreadsheet as the next step in our computation. The formula for this transformation is as follows: =RANK(AB2,$AB$2:$AB$112,1). Recall that the number of qualifying stocks in the spreadsheet changes daily according to market action. Thus, the number 112 in the formula signifies that at the time of this writing there were 112 qualifying stocks in my spreadsheet. All of the other applications of RANK statistics in the spreadsheet have been adjusted correspondingly. Next this formula is inserted into cell BE2 and dragged down the BE column.

As a final step in the computation of the Future Trend Index, combine the Residual Ranking (Rr) with the Universal Index Ranking (UIr) using the following formula: AP2+BE2. This formula is then inserted into cell BF2 and dragged down the BF column. Label the BF column FTI to signify that it contains the Future Trend Index.

a) To implement this strategy, first compute the Future Trend Index and insert it into column BF of your spreadsheet as described above.
b) Next go to the Future Trend Index (FTI) in column BF and sort this column from largest to smallest values, with the largest values at the top. Focus attention on the top ten stocks in the column.
c) For ancillary confirmation it is helpful next to look at the Universal Index Ranking in column BE of your spreadsheet. There it is helpful to choose the two or three stocks with the highest Universal Index Ranking (UIr) values from among the ten stocks identified earlier.
d) Final selection can be made by choosing those remaining stocks with the smallest percentage lag in column F and/or the highest Multiple Ratio Index (MRI) value in column BC.

Currently, I am finding the Future Trend Strategy to be especially beneficial for several reasons. It appears that reliance on the Future Trend Index in particular helps to identify stocks that have longer persistence as winners and thus the frequency and number of trades required to maintain a healthy portfolio can be greatly reduced. At the same time, other performance indices such as the Universal Index can be helpful to identify those stocks that have the best global performance record and can be considered as a starting point in stock selection.

Strategies Compared

It is one thing to propose a number of trading strategies as has been done for you in this chapter. It is quite another thing to find out if the strategies actually work to produce profits. To test these ten strategies I created ten different portfolios on February 28, 2015. The strategies are each designed to pick the top two or three stocks; however, for comparison purposes it seemed best to choose the top five stocks by each strategy to form the ten different portfolios. This expansion to five stocks for each portfolio also minimized the overlap between portfolios and enabled more reliable comparison. Each of the ten portfolios consisted of ten thousand dollars divided equally among the five stocks selected by a particular strategy; i.e., two thousand dollars per stock.

Because these are short-term swing trading strategies, it seemed adequate to test the portfolio performance over one week. Table 10.1 below summarizes the performance for each strategy by comparison with major market averages for the five-day trading week from February 28 through March 6, 2015.

TABLE 10.1. Ten Trading Strategies Compared for Performance over One Week, Two Weeks, and Five Weeks (2/28/15-4/3/15)

Trading Strategy	Percentage Gain (Loss)		
Momentum Strategies	One Week	Two Weeks	Five Weeks
1. The Percentage Lag Strategy	4.84	7.88	0.26
2. The One-Month Momentum Strategy	0.32	2.35	11.72
3. The Cumulative Momentum Strategy	0.37	3.78	10.76
4. The Multiple-Ratio Momentum Strategy	(-2.15)	1.90	5.14
5. The Patterned Price Movement Strategy	(-1.06)	1.55	10.70
Performance Strategies			
6. The One-Month Gain Strategy	0.44	3.19	11.01
7. The Universal Index Strategy	1.20	2.68	12.12
8. The Global Total Performance Strategy	(-1.16)	1.12	6.45
9. The Comprehensive Performance Strategy	(-0.44)	2.34	6.50
10. The Future Trend Strategy	1.26	2.17	14.37
Major Indices			
11. The S&P 500 Index	(-1.56)	(-2.49)	(-1.64)
12. The Dow Jones Industrial Average	(-1.52)	(-2.16)	(-2.04)

Notice in Table 10.1 that even though the comparison period lasted only five weeks, and despite the fact that the trial weeks came during a period when the major indices were in a downtrend, all of the trading strategies outperformed the major indices during that period. The one strategy that failed to outperform the major indices in the first week was the Multiple-Ratio Momentum Strategy. In defense of that strategy it should be observed that it is the most volatile of the proposed strategies. This means that it is expected to exceed the indices to the positive side in an uptrend, just as it did to the negative side in a downtrend. And it is evident that this strategy outperformed the major averages in the second week (1.90%) and in the overall period (5.14%).

You will note that the Percentage Lag Strategy was the best performing strategy for this trial period after two weeks (7.88%), but that it became the worst performing strategy after five weeks (0.26%). This outcome is consistent with a swing trading style that seldom holds a stock for more than three weeks. Following the recommended rules for selling stocks with percentage lag above four percent would have preserved the higher gains over the full trading period.

To reach my goal of 10% gain per month, I need to realize about 2.3% gain per week. To compensate and allow for the fact that the overall market was in a downtrend, we can say that I need to exceed the overall average of the S&P 500 Index by an average amount of 2.2% per week. To accomplish this in the first trial week I would have needed to gain about 0.62% and in the second trial week I would have needed to gain about 0.93% for a cumulative gain of 1.91%. Note that all but three of the ten strategies attained this high goal; i.e., the Multiple-Ratio Momentum Strategy (1.90%), the Patterned Price Movement Strategy (1.55%), and the Global Total Performance Strategy (1.12%).

In defense of the underperforming strategies it should be noted that each strategy was designed to pick the best one or two stocks in the universe of stocks. For computational purposes the trial admitted the best five stocks for inclusion into each portfolio. This added inclusiveness no doubt weakened performance and caused the result to more nearly approximate the results of the major averages. In addition, following the initial stock selection, no trades were permitted during the trial period. Thus the trial results may well be more conservative than normally would be the case. Admittedly this was a rough and dirty comparison, but I fully intend to continue on a weekly basis with successive reselection of stocks to see how the strategies perform in a variety of market conditions.

Summary:

In the last two chapters we have considered ten different trading strategies based on the indices generated earlier in your spreadsheet. Five of these strategies are termed "momentum" strategies, and five are "performance" strategies as defined operationally in the chapters. Each strategy involves the use of a primary index supplemented by two or more ancillary indices for reliable selection of stocks. Because these strategies are expected to differ in their profitability under different market conditions, the reader is encouraged to experiment with each of them to find those strategies most productive at any given time.

A five-week trial was conducted to compare the strategies in their performance with one another and with the major market averages. The Percentage Lag Strategy was found to be the most profitable of the strategies in this brief trial after two weeks under adverse market conditions. The Future Trend Strategy appeared to be the most profitable strategy after five weeks. All ten of the strategies were found to outperform the major averages, and it was shown to be possible to reach a targeted trading goal of ten percent gain per month with seven of the ten strategies under similar market conditions. With refinements in the predictor variables detailed in Chapter Thirteen, it is expected that results of such trading strategies will be even more successful in the future.

PART FIVE

Market Timing and Leveraging

In the following two chapters we turn attention to market timing and leveraging.

Even if we are able to identify the best stocks for investment at any given time, it is still important to know when to be fully invested in those stocks and when to be out of the market altogether. And once our trading strategies become consistently profitable for us, it is useful to know how to leverage our investments so as to get maximum returns. Chapter Eleven introduces four new technical timing indicators that were not discussed earlier because they are not readily quantifiable as those earlier indicators were. And once our trading strategies become consistently profitable for us, it is useful to know how to leverage our investments so as to get maximum returns. This then becomes the focus of Chapter Twelve.

CHAPTER 11

Timing Indicators

> "To everything there is a season, a time for every purpose under heaven: ... a time to gain, and a time to lose; a time to keep, and a time to throw away."
> — Ecclesiastes 3:1,6

Up to this point in this book we have examined how a number of technical and fundamental indices can be generated to rank stocks in an Excel spreadsheet and how these indices may be used in actual short-term trading strategies. In this chapter we will look more closely at timing indicators so that we can make better decisions about when to buy and sell. To some extent when we rank stocks according to technical indicators, we are already making timing decisions. It may very well be the case that the technical indicators presented earlier encompass the same timing information that we shall explore in this chapter. Nevertheless those technical indicators tell us little about overall market timing conditions, and there are even more explicit methods than those we have encountered so far for timing individual stocks.

This chapter will be controversial—especially for extreme random walk theorists who believe that it is not possible to time the market. By contrast, I agree with Ben Stein (2004) who titled one of his books, "Yes, You Can Time the Market," and with William O'Neil (1995) who wrote that knowing when to be in the market and when to be out of the market is one of the keys to investment success. However, even if the majority of traders and investors might agree that it is possible to time the market, there is little if any agreement about how this can be accomplished. Maturi (1993) presented 100 different market timing systems that have been popular with various persons at various times. However, many of those systems, such as measuring women's hemlines and counting solar flares, are not very satisfying empirically.

The position in this book is that successful timing systems may be of two general types. There are macro timing indicators that tell us when the major averages can be expected to rise or fall, and there are micro timing indicators that dictate when it may be most appropriate to buy or sell individual stocks. Both are important. We will deal here with macro timing indicators first.

Macro Timing Indicators

It can be useful to know in a probabilistic sense when the overall market is likely to go up and when it is likely to go down. This kind of knowledge is attainable—at least to the extent that it can be profitably actionable.

PE Averages and RSI Averages

Stein (2004) gave practical contrarian guidelines when he wrote that the best time to buy is when overall market PE averages are at a relative low, and that the best time to sell is when overall market PE averages are at a relative high. The historical market average PE is 16.6, and at the time of this writing the average PE is high at around 26.3 by the latest adjusted computations. Bear in mind, however, that PE varies widely by market sector, so this information is not particularly useful in judging individual stocks. No doubt it is useful to the long-term investor who is buying index funds or reliable mutual funds, but it is not precise enough for the short-term trader who may be trading individual stocks or index options.

Related to Stein's proposed methodology, it is possible to employ the Excel command AVERAGE to obtain successive averages of the relative strength index in your own database on a weekly basis. When the RSI average reaches a comparative low, one can gather confidence that a market bottom is near and it may be safer to make long purchases. Admittedly this approach lacks precision because the particular composition of stocks in your database will be in constant transition. It is also possible, however, to apply the RSI to major indices for equities to determine overall market direction. Thus for example, an RSI above 70 on the S&P500 Index may suggest that the market is nearing a downward correction—especially if there is a divergence between rising RSI values and leveling or falling index averages.

VIX Trends and Put/Call Ratios

A more precise method can be found by using the S&P 500 Volatility Index (VIX) or by using put/call ratios. It turns out that these two approaches are redundant; that is, they lead to the exact same useful market timing conclusions, as I demonstrated in my earlier trading book (Henning, 2010). There I also presented a summary of five years of VIX data to demonstrate that the market goes through regular cycles averaging about 49 days. Subsequently, I have found that the cycles have narrowed somewhat and that S&P 500 uptrends last longer on average (42 days) than downtrends (30 days). However, the standard deviations associated with these averages are so high that the averages can present enough precision for timing decisions only when they are used in conjunction with the VIX. In practice, when it is found that the VIX has reached a relative peak or valley that comes at the time estimated through cycle averaging, one can then gather confidence that a new trend cycle has begun. The exact procedure is spelled out in greater detail in my earlier book for any who may be interested. Since writing about those observable market phenomena, I have not subsequently found that approach to have lost any of its dependability or predictive accuracy.

In that book I showed how traders could realize gains in excess of 300 percent per year by attending to these market cycles and investing in leveraged bear funds during downtrends and leveraged bull funds during uptrends. My goal here is not to repeat what is already available in the earlier book for any reader who may be interested. It is enough here to assert that market timing is possible and that the rewards can be substantial.

Admittedly such macro timing information is more useful to investors in mutual funds or index funds than to traders of individual stocks because individual stocks may often be largely unaffected by major market trends. It may also be useful to traders of index options who want to be sure that they are on the right side of a trend. For traders of individual stocks, however, it can be shown that individual stocks are not always responsive to major market trends. It seems that there is always profit to be made with individual stocks in any market trend if the trader has done the necessary homework. For example, even during the steep market downturn associated with the terrorist attacks of September 11, 2001, airport security stocks had a positive run. Therefore, let us turn our attention now to micro timing indicators that may be more relevant for traders of individual stocks. Happily many of the micro timing indicators may also be applied to major market indices and in that way serve as macro timing indicators as well.

Micro Timing Indicators

Many books have already been written by market technicians who offer advice about how to time the price movements of individual stocks and thus how to find optimal times for buying and selling. Several of those books are in the list of recommended readings at the back of this book (e.g., Grimes, 2012; McAllen, 2012; and Murphy, 1999). Many of these timing technicians may be classified under the rubric of "chartists." That is, they are focused on patterns of price movement that become visible in the charts. They look for patterns predictive of future price direction, such as *double bottoms, head and shoulders* formations, and *cup and handle* figures. Decisions of when to buy and sell are then based on matching price movement patterns to a repertoire of such formations. Often such decisions are successful. For that reason it is important to become conversant with that approach.

Unfortunately, however, frequently such decisions are not successful. Part of the problem is that recognition of a pattern is subjectively determined, and therefore not everyone is in agreement whether a given pattern has occurred. Furthermore, as any honest technician will confess, even when there is some consensus about pattern occurrence, the desired results do not always follow. For example, there are instances when a supposed *double bottom* did not predict an upward trend reversal, but instead became a precursor to a continuing downward slide.

Other technicians focus primarily on timing signals provided by special indexes such as the Relative Strength Index (RSI), the Average Directional Index (ADX), and the Moving Average Convergence/Divergence Oscillator

(MACD). Although this may represent an improvement over mere attempts at pattern recognition, here too the landscape is dotted with the wreckage of decisions gone awry. For this reason, the most successful technical decisions will rely on confirmation from multiple indicators.

In this section we will consider four tried and true micro timing indicators. In order to benefit most from this discussion, you will find it helpful to go to Stockcharts.com and call up a "sharpchart" for an individual stock of interest. Beneath the chart in the area designated "indicators" it will be important to add one additional indicator labeled "ADX Line (w/+DI and –DI)." Then click on "Update" at the top of the chart. You should then be looking at a picture that is similar to that of Figure 11.1 below. The fact that such valuable charts are available online to everyone free of charge explains why StockCharts.com is one of my favorite and most frequented web sites.

Figure 11.1. Finviz SharpChart Representation of INUV on May 15, 2015, with Critical Timing Indicators Depicted (Courtesy of StockCharts.com). (Note, be sure to log in to the website in case the colors are not reproduced in this printing.)

Notice that the company Inovo (INUV) had a highly profitable run in its stock (it tripled in value) during one three-month period represented in the chart. In this chart we can see four timing indicators that provide signals that serve to enhance profitable decision making. Those indicators are found respectively from top to bottom (1) in the Relative Strength Index (RSI) trend line, (2) in the volume indicator histogram, (3) in the MACD histogram, and (4) in the ADX trend lines. Let us consider these indicator signals in order from top to bottom.

1. The Relative Strength Index (RSI) Trend Line

Observe the RSI trend line near the top of the chart. Traditional practice dictated by Wilder (1978) for use with commodities would dictate that whenever the RSI value exceeds 70, it is time to sell, and whenever the RSI value falls to 30 or below, it is time to buy. If you had followed these guidelines strictly for this stock, you would never have purchased it, and you would have missed a great buying opportunity. Or if you already owned the stock, you would have sold at RSI 70 around 3/5 and missed almost the entire run up in the stock price. Based on this single example selected at random we can reject the traditional guidelines out of hand.

However, you can see that whenever the line begins to ascend from below the 70 mark, there is a corresponding ascent in the stock price chart below the RSI chart. This was apparent on the dates of 1/25, 2/3, 2/26, 3/14, 4/1, and 5/12. You can see that the most seminal of ascending movements took place when the line crossed above the 50 mark as on 1/25, 2/26, and 5/12. It is important to identify upward breakout points as early as possible in their trajectory. Otherwise a buy signal is no better than a lagging indicator. The point here is that, if you had purchased the stock at any one of the three seminal buy signals, you would have realized a profit. It would appear from this limited one-stock example, that it is far better to purchase a stock at the point of an RSI crossover at the 50 mark than to look for stocks bottoming at the RSI 30 mark to buy or crossing above the 70 mark to sell.

Sell signals are most profitably interpreted as downward crossings from above to below the 70 mark—especially after an extended period above 70. By this criterion the only two sell signals were issued on 4/1 and 4/16. However, it appears that 4/1 was too ephemeral to be helpful and 4/16 was too late to spare us much pain.

2. The Volume Indicator Histogram

At the bottom of the price movement chart in the middle of Figure 11.1 you can see the volume histogram. Whenever the histogram spikes upward with gray bars, it shows a surge in buy volume. Whenever the histogram spikes upward with pink bars, it shows a surge in sell volume. Conventional wisdom would dictate that in order to constitute a buy signal there must be a surge in buy volume that is comparatively high—much higher than preceding buy volume surges. You can see in Figure 11.1 that such volume buy signals were registered on or about the following dates: 2/4, 3/2, 3/28, 4/4, and 5/13. The most salient of these buy volume spikes took place on 4/4 and 5/13 after much of the price rises had already been registered. Furthermore, each of the candidate buy volume spikes occurred within a few days after an RSI signal. From this we may infer that volume is a lagging indicator of price movement for buying opportunities. At best it serves to confirm buy decisions made on the basis of other signals.

We may interpret selling volume spikes on 4/1, 4/12, 4/19, and 5/17 in the same way, as signals to sell. Certainly 4/12 and 4/19 were reflective of price downturns, but only 4/12 qualified as a profitable leading indicator. Interestingly, the 4/12 spike in sell volume is one of the few clear timing indicators that would have spared traders from the precipitous price downturn that followed shortly thereafter.

3. The Moving Average Convergence/Divergence (MACD) Histogram and Moving Average Crossovers

The blue histogram in the Moving Average Convergence/Divergence (MACD) portion of Figure 11.1 provides information that is somewhat redundant of the information provided by the moving average lines in the same diagram. This is because the histogram represents the degree of separation between the two exponential moving average (EMA) lines. Notice that when the black (fast) 12-day moving average line is above the red (slow) 26-day moving average line, the histogram bars are in positive territory above the zero or central point. When the red (slow) moving average line is above the black (fast) moving average line, the histogram bars are in negative territory below the zero point. The height or depth of the bars corresponds to the degree of separation between the two moving average lines. As the degree of separation increases, the amount of momentum is said to increase, whether downward or upward momentum. It is apparent that whenever the histogram bars are in the mode of stair-stepping upward progression, the price of the stock is also in ascent, and the reverse is true whenever the histogram is progressively descending. Critical buy signals are said to occur whenever the histogram progresses upward from the zero point, which corresponds exactly with those times that the fast (black) line crosses above the red (slow) line. In the case of Figure 11.1 those signals occurred on or about the following dates: 1/24, 3/1, and 5/13.

Conversely, critical sell signals are said to occur whenever the histogram descends down across the zero point, which also coincides with those times that the fast (black) moving average line crosses downwards over the slow (red) moving average line. In Figure 11.1 we can see that those sell signals occurred on 2/23 and 4/18—too late to avoid the losses incurred by negative price action.

However, if in Figure 11.1 we had sold INUV stock on 4/13 right at the time the histogram began its downward progression after a high climb, we could have avoided the price correction that began on 4/17. It is clear from this example that the histogram progression provides earlier signals than either moving average crossovers or histogram crossovers. This is especially the case after the histogram has already made an unusually high ascent or an unusually low descent. By adding this additional histogram rule, we can see that 4/13 constituted an early sell signal and 4/27 and 5/11 provided additional early buy signals. My conclusion is that MACD is indeed a powerful timing indicator, but only if we attend to the histogram progressions and do not wait for the EMA line crossovers.

4. The ADX Trend Lines

At the bottom of Figure 11.1 we can see a graph of the three ADX trend lines that were also developed by Wilder (1978) for use with commodities trading. The three lines are labeled as follows: the Average Directional Index (ADX) is the black line, the Minus Directional Indicator (-DI) is the red line, and the Plus Directional Indicator (+DI) is the green line. Notice that the black (ADX) line is representative of the overall trend strength without regard to trend direction in the stock price. The red and green lines represent opposing ends of the trend direction continuum. A rising green line (+DM) is associated with rising positive direction in the stock price, as is a falling red line (-DM). Conversely, a rising red line and a falling green line depict growing downward direction. Traditionally according to Wilder buy signals are given when the green line crosses up over the red line, but only when the black line itself is trending upward. Wilder stipulated that the ADX line should be above 25 as a requirement for a buy signal. Many traders now use 20 as the critical level. By this rule, ADX buy signals were issued as green line crossovers above the red line with sufficiently high black line on or about the following dates: 1/29, 2/28, and 4/28. ADX buy signals were issued as green line crossovers above the red line on or about the following dates: 1/29, 2/28, and 4/29. Note that all three of these red line crossovers occurred at a time when the black line was still trending downward, but they each provided early indication of a forthcoming black line trend reversal.

Timing Indicators Compared

If we compare these four timing indicators with respect to buy and sell signals based on the chart of price action in Figure 11.1, we can see which signals were most accurate and timely. This comparison is summarized in Table 11.1 below.

TABLE 11.1. Signal Dates for Buy and Sell Decisions with Four Timing Indicators

Indicator	Buy	Sell
RSI	1/25, 2/3*, 2/26*, 5/12*	4/1, 4/16
Volume	2/4*, 3/2, 3/28, 4/4*, 5/13*	4/1, 4/12*, 4/19, 5/17
MACD	1/24*, 3/1, 4/27, 5/11*, 5/13*	2/23, 4/13*, 4/18
ADX	1/29, 2/28*, 4/29	2/25, 4/23

*Indicates profitable signals.

Admittedly this comparison suffers from limitations—chiefest among which is the fact that it is based on results from only one stock chart. Nevertheless, we have gathered some useful information that is summarized in Table 11.1. First of all, it is apparent that all of the timing indicators leave much to be desired as sell signals. Usually they are too late to the party to serve for purposes of damage control. Price declines appear to be too sudden and precipitous for our timing signals to catch them before the fact. There are two notable exceptions to this observation; i.e., when there is a huge spike in sell volume as indicated by the volume histogram (4/12), and when the MACD histogram begins a downward progression from a high positive peak (4/13). Examining the price action in Figure 11.1, we can see that the actual most critical times to sell would have been 12/30, 2/17, and 4/13, and as noted, only the last of these times was captured by two of the signals.

On the buy side of the ledger, we can see again from the price action in Figure 11.1 that the actual most critical times to buy occurred on 1/20, 2/4, 2/25, 4/2, and 5/12. There was a price spike on 4/29, but it was of such short duration that only day traders could have benefited. The MACD crossover on 1/24 was the only actionable signal for the 1/20 event although it was a few days later than optimal. The 2/4 event was captured by only the RSI (2/3) and the volume histogram (2/4). The 2/25 event was captured by only the RSI (2/26) and the ADX crossover (2/28)–although the ADX crossover was a bit later than desirable. The 4/2 event was captured by only the volume histogram (4/4). The 5/12 event was captured by three indicators: the RSI (5/12), the volume histogram (5/13), and the MACD histogram progression (5/13).

These results argue for the need to seek confirmation from multiple timing signals. For sell decisions I can depend only on sell spikes in the volume histogram and downward progressions from peaks of the MACD histogram. For buy decisions, RSI jumps upward from 70, buy volume spikes in the volume histogram, and MACD crossovers are all useful indicators. The ADX indicator appeared to be the weakest signal source. Perhaps it is more useful with other types of stocks, or possibly it could be improved upon by incorporating green line crossovers above and below the ADX trend line and not focusing exclusively on green line crossovers of the red line.

Summary:

In this chapter we have considered four timing indicators that could profitably be used to complement the stock rankings provided in earlier chapters. Specifically, we have considered the Relative Strength Index (RSI), the Trading Volume Histogram, the Moving Average Convergence/Divergence (MACD) Indicator, and the Average Directional Index (ADX) for buy and sell timing signals. Based on the price action of a single stock taken as an example, it was concluded that use of a variety of timing indicators for buy decisions is recommended. The RSI, the Volume Histogram, the MACD crossover, and the MACD histogram upward progression from bottoms were all potentially useful timing indicators when properly applied. For sell decisions, only the sell volume histogram and the MACD histogram downward progression from peaks were useful. Other sell signals may serve as confirmatory lagging indicators, but are often too late to protect from sudden losses. Of course, none of these timing indicators is intended to replace ranking information provided in earlier chapters. At best the signals can improve timing decisions for purchases and sales dictated by the rankings. These findings are tentative due to sample limitations.

CHAPTER 12

LEVERAGE

> "There is a severe evil which I have seen under the
> sun: riches kept for their owner to his hurt. But
> those riches perish through misfortune."
> — ECCLESIASTES 5:13,14

It is by intention that this discussion of leverage comes near the end of the book. This is because leverage is not something a trader should think about until after a regular pattern of successful trading has been established. Leveraging has the great advantage of enabling possible multiplied earnings beyond what could normally be expected given a limited amount of investment capital. But leveraging has the profound disadvantage of multiplying losses beyond what would normally have been expected had the trader not resorted to leveraging in the first place. In short, use of leveraging can result in both multiplied gains and multiplied losses. It can be used both to capitalize on risk and to mitigate risk. That is why some understanding of the nature of risk is central to the proper use of leveraging.

Risk

Some experts have mistakenly equated risk to volatility. While it is true that volatility may introduce some elements of risk, the nature of risk is much more profound and pervasive than mere volatility. As Berenstein (1996) so skillfully notes, "Risk touches on the most profound aspects of psychology, mathematics, statistics, and history." The story of our lives as individuals and of modern civilization collectively is a history of the development of risk management. Without such management modern finance, medicine, space travel, insurance, education and economics would not be possible. And yet, as Ferguson (2008) and others accurately point out, our efforts at risk mitigation have also brought us the welfare state, business monopolies, and political corruption. As a result also we now have an entire generation that believes they have a right to health insurance, to government paid disability, to higher minimum wage, to redistribution of the incomes of others, and to subsidized food and housing. Indeed, as Prime Minister Margaret Thatcher once observed, "Socialism is a great system, as long as other people's money lasts." But in our generation we have, temporarily at least, found ways to make socialism last on the fumes of leverage long after all the money is all gone.

My point is simply that use of leverage can be a very dangerous activity, particularly when it is practiced by the state. Banks and other financial institutions often exercise leverage far beyond the levels permitted to individuals. Presumably this is because it is assumed that such institutions have greater wisdom than individuals in the disposition of resources, or that their use of leverage is for some greater good. Although use of leverage can be highly advantageous to the individual trader when necessary precautions are taken, the perils of using leverage need to be fully understood. Do not think that you are exempted from the dangers of leverage by your exceptional intelligence. It is well known, for example, that no less brilliant a financial scholar than John Maynard Keynes managed to lose three-fourths of his substantial net worth by trading stocks and commodities on margin, even during the bull market of the roaring twenties (Ahamed, 2009). Years later, however, he was able to recoup most of his losses through more circumspect trading.

Using Margin

One of the most common ways traders can take advantage of leverage is through the use of margin in their brokerage accounts. Those traders who qualify--typically with a brokerage account holding a minimum of two thousand dollars--may borrow the equivalent of their capital holdings for reinvestment in approved stocks or other approved investment instruments. Thus, if you have ten thousand dollars or equivalent holdings in a margin account, you may be eligible to purchase up to twenty thousand dollars in total approved equity holdings. Understandably, if you are so positioned, it can be very gratifying to discover that, if your stocks have risen five percent in value in one day, you have actually gained ten percent on your invested capital in terms of in real disposable income. As you can imagine, the potential for compounding and accelerating earnings is truly mind-boggling.

At the same time, use of margin has its drawbacks. The foremost drawback is that margin can make your losses also compound in reverse. So that, if you are fully margined and if your stocks lose five percent of their value, you are in reality losing ten percent of your investment capital. Equally daunting is the fact that, if your losses mount to the degree that you no longer hold at least 35 percent equity in your account, you will receive a dreaded margin call that will force you either to liquidate stocks or to deposit more money in your account. Unfortunately, if you must liquidate stocks, you are often compelled to sell them at a loss during a low point in their price cycle. If this were not bad enough, you also must pay interest on the money you borrow from your broker for reinvestment. Some brokerage houses during some market periods make more money from margin interest than they do from commissions or any other source.

There is one other drawback to trading on margin that some people do not consider. Brokerage houses are able to dictate which stocks you are allowed to purchase on margin and what percentage of the stock purchase price you will be allowed to borrow. It often happens that the best stocks for you to purchase are stocks that the brokerage houses have determined according to their own secret formulae are too risky for you to purchase on margin. Thus, you will not be able to borrow money to purchase those stocks. For that reason you should always check with your brokerage margin web page before purchasing any stock on margin to see to what extent that particular stock may in fact be marginable.

Leveraged Bull and Bear Funds

Another way for traders to exercise leverage is through leveraged bull and bear funds. By purchasing such funds a trader may obtain greater leverage than is obtainable through the use of margin alone. Unlike the case with margin trading, it may not be necessary to hold a minimum balance to qualify for this leverage, there is no requirement to pay margin interest, and there is no such thing as a margin call for such investments. In a few cases it can even be possible to purchase a portion of such leveraged funds on margin and thereby extend leverage to an even greater degree.

There are two general types of such leveraged funds: mutual funds and exchange-traded funds (ETFs). Of these two types of funds, ETFs have the advantage for the trader that they can be traded intraday and they have no fees or balance minimums. Mutual funds are traded at the closing price once each day and require a minimum balance plus management fees. Typically all such funds are based on the movement of some underlying equity or commodity index and "ultra" funds may seek to move two or three times the movement of that index in a positive (bullish) or in a negative (bearish) direction.

My personal favorite leveraged funds are based on the S&P 500 Volatility Index (VIX) and therefore they tend to extend gains beyond what is possible with other "ultra" funds inasmuch as the VIX tends to rise and fall to a greater extent than other indices. In particular, TVIX is an ETF of interest during bearish market conditions, and SVIX is an ETF of interest during bullish market conditions. The fund companies that offer such funds are able to make money for themselves because their risk is balanced through the offering of a bear fund to complement an equivalent bull fund. Of course they also make money through the generous spreads (the differences between bid and ask prices) that they can set in the trading of their funds.

Options

The purchasing of *call* and *put* options is probably the way in which a trader can obtain the greatest amount of leverage for his or her investment capital. It is also possible to sell options on equities that you already own and in that way to "rent out" your stocks. But that procedure does not involve much risk, much leverage, or much financial gain. Option trading has become a highly complex and highly rewarding activity, although it has been acknowledged that 90 percent of all option traders lose money. It will not be possible in this book to provide a thorough treatment of option trading strategies, but I highly recommend other resources such as Binnewies (1995) and Fulman (1992) referenced in the back of this book.

Although the leveraging possibilities are truly great through the trading of options, there are several drawbacks in such trading. First, unlike equities, options expire after a set period of time. Because the clock is ticking on any option investment, you are hoping that the market will move in your favor within the holding period. Often that does not happen. Another drawback is that commissions for the trading of options tend to be somewhat higher than commissions for the trading of stocks. For me, the most frustrating drawback is that, because options are traded on a supply and demand basis, option values do not always move in lock step with the underlying equity or index. For example, the underlying index may move upward in value while the option remains flat.

There are many different kinds of options and option trading strategies. Options can be used both to take advantage of volatility and to hedge against volatility. They can be purchased both singly and in combinations with other options and equities. It is important to read extensively and then to use extensive practice with simulated trading before committing financial resources to the trading of options.

Summary

This chapter has consisted of a discussion of some of the advantages and disadvantages of leverage. We have seen how leverage may be employed through the use of margin trading, by purchasing leveraged bull and bear funds, and through the trading of options. It was recommended that extensive additional reading and simulated trading be undertaken before launching out into the trading of options.

CHAPTER 13

AFTERTHOUGHTS AND WRAPPING UP

> "Let us hear the conclusion of the whole matter: fear God and keep His commandments, for this is man's all."
> — ECCLESIASTES 12:13

We have covered a lot of ground in this little book. And yet I need to mention several important matters in this chapter in order to achieve a measure of closure. Some of these remaining matters are practical instructions that need to be provided in order for the approach to stock analysis described earlier to work effectively. I call these "housekeeping issues." Some of the remaining matters consist of a list of recent insights that occurred to me in the process of writing this book. They are sufficiently important for me to share them here in this way, and it appeared to be too difficult for me at this stage to go back and incorporate them in some earlier chapters. Some of the remaining matters involve a kind of "wish list" of topics for research needed. Hopefully some enterprising graduate students will take up the banner and undertake the required effort to find appropriate answers to the questions and solutions to the problems. And finally, I need to back off and provide a kind of overview perspective on the matters presented in this book as a find of farewell conclusion.

Housekeeping Issues

No doubt some questions will arise in the process of implementing the system of data analysis described in this book. Here I will try to anticipate some of these questions.

1. What should be done about missing data?

You have likely discovered by this time that some of the data needed for entry into your Excel spreadsheet are not available. One popular convention in the social sciences is to substitute the mean of the distribution of any variable into the cells where missing data occur. In this way it is hoped that biases can be eliminated. That works very well for some variables such as *beta* where the mean of the distribution is known to be 1.00 by design. But here we are dealing with so many variables with so many different distributions that vary each day that it is too onerous to compute means for each of them repetitively. For some of these variables the mean of the distribution is not even the best approximation to use for missing data. For example, profit margin is one variable that often has missing data. For that variable I have found that the value available for return on assets provides a better approximation to use for missing data than the distribution mean. For price-to-sales ratio (PSR), when that datum is missing, the stock usually has negative fundamentals overall. Therefore, I routinely enter a negative value that is 10 times the return on assets (resulting in a positive value) as a quantity that is a better approximation than the distribution mean. Similarly, when five-year sales growth data are not available, the quantity minus ten (-10.0) usually provides a useful approximation. Those examples cover nearly all of the missing data you may encounter.

2. How often should data be updated?

As noted in the early chapters of this book, some data must be updated in their entirety at the end of each trading day. These include the stock price, the 52-week high, the 52-week low, and the relative strength index (RSI) value. Other information must also be added at the end of each trading day, but only for those stocks that are being newly added to the database. This new daily information includes all of the technical and fundamental and data for each new stock. In addition, because the total number of stocks in your database will vary from day to day, it is necessary to enter a corrected total for every column for which rank statistics are generated as well as for the cells where correlation and regression statistics are calculated.

Other information changes so infrequently that it is not necessary to make corrections daily. For example, the key fundamental information can be edited weekly or monthly, and then only for the top third of the stocks in the database. For the universal index (UI) it is useful to check each of the component variables monthly to see if they are still contributing effectively to the discrimination in ranks, or if they need to be replaced.

3. What may be the most suitable criteria for adding and deleting stocks from the database?

For adding new stocks to your database, originally I proposed that one should go to both Finviz.Com and Stockcharts.Com and find those stocks rising in value by at least 30 percent over the past three months and rising ten percent over the past month. It now appears more efficient to look for only those stocks rising in price by 20 percent over the past month. From among these 20 percent risers, it is still important to look for those stocks with prices holding within three percent of their 52-week highs. It is also important to concentrate only on those stocks that have risen at least 50 percent from their 52-week lows. Thus, stocks should have values of 1.5 or above in the multiple column. Be careful not to include stocks with a price plateau caused by acquisition or merger. Such stocks no longer exhibit upward momentum.

For deleting stocks from your database, eliminate any stocks whose multiple values drop below 1.5. Also, remove stocks whose combined one-plus-three-month gain is less than 30 percent. If this still leaves you with an unmanageable number of stocks in your database, say above 120, you can consider eliminating stocks with negative momentum ratios (MRIs) that will be discussed in the next section. Another useful deletion criterion is a Universal Index (UI) value below -9.0. In bull market seasons when there is an overabundance of stocks in the database, this UI criterion can be moved to -8.0.

4. How dependable are internet data sources?

This question has caused me some agony over the years. It is apparent to any objective observer that vastly different levels of accuracy are provided by different purveyors of market data. For example, on the day of this writing I consulted three different websites for data concerning the stock *Revolution Lighting* (RVLT). Yahoo Finance reported the *beta* value of that stock as 8.03, but Finviz.Com reported that value as 3.75 on the same day. Finviz.Com reported the relative strength index (RSI) for RVLT as 38.62, but Stockcharts.Com reported that value as 39.88 on the same day. For the honest researcher this is frustrating to say the least. There seems to be very little accountability for accuracy in this arena. At the same time, some kinds of information, such as closing price, 52-week high, and 52-week low, seem highly dependable everywhere. If there was ever a need for consumer protection, it is in the area of financial data provision. Over time, however, one can develop a sense of which sites are dependable for which kinds of information and which sites are not at all dependable for some kinds of critical information.

Recent Insights

A number of important insights have occurred to me in the course of writing this book. Unfortunately some of them did not come to me early enough to be incorporated into the earlier chapters. In this section you will find a list of those ideas that you may wish to consider in your own financial engineering endeavors.

Interval Gains Ranking

At the beginning of this writing project I considered the primary criterion for variable selection to be significant and meaningful correlation with one-month gain. It seemed logical that, if the goal is to create a model that ranks stocks in accordance with growth potential, it would be wise to include only those prediction variables that exhibited a high correlation with one-month growth. Later I added correlates of three-month growth to accommodate the fact that fundamental variables may not change appreciably in a one-month period because earnings may be reported on a quarterly basis. This correlational approach was effective, even though as I pointed out earlier, equities data do not entirely satisfy the assumptions underlying the application of parametric statistics (i.e., normal and independent distribution) and therefore correlation may not be the most appropriate statistical procedure to use.

However, it later occurred to me that "interval gains ranking" could be an alternative procedure for variable selection in model building. This is a simple four-step procedure to select the most useful variables and variable combinations for ranking stocks.

1. The first step is to choose a time interval of interest. The easiest interval to implement is one day.
2. Next, at the close of trading on any given day go through all of the stocks in your database and mark those stocks that have gained two percent or more that day with a caret (^) at the end of each symbol.
3. Now go through each prediction variable and combination variable of interest one by one, sorting stocks from the most desirable to the least desirable on that variable.
4. With each sort, tally the number of stocks with carets (^) that fall into the top 15 ranks. By this procedure, the best predictors will be those variables that consistently have the most stocks with carets in the top 15 positions.

New Prediction Variables

Using the Interval Gains Ranking procedure described above, I have found several new prediction variables that are more powerful than some of the original group of predictors that were incorporated into the Universal Index (UI) in Chapter Eight. Accordingly, I have revised my Universal Index components in ways that I plan to divulge in this section. Here for your consideration is a list of these recently identified prediction variables.

1. The Momentum Ratio Index (MRI)
   One of the most powerful new growth-prediction variables I have found is one that I have labeled the Momentum Ratio Index (MRI). It is calculated by simply dividing the number of times a stock price has multiplied from its 52-week low (Mult) by the percentage lag (%Lag) of the current stock price below the 52-week high. Of all the variables I follow, this one has been consistently the highest in the number of stocks with daily price rises above two percent that fall in the top fifteen ranks. The Excel formula for computation and insertion into the top data cell of your MRI column is as follows: =X2/Y2, where X is the column holding the Mult variable values and Y is the column holding the %Lag values. This cell must then be copied into the top data cell of your MRI column and dragged down through all the rows in your data set. Because of the predictive power of this new variable, it is a great candidate for inclusion into a revised and more powerful Universal Index (UI).
2. The Multiple Lag Ratio (MLR)
   Yet another powerful new index that is worthy of inclusion into a revised and more powerful Universal Index (UI) may be entitled the Multiple Lag Ratio (MLR). This variable is a variant of the Momentum Ratio Index described above. The formula for computation of the MLR is as follows: =(X2/2)/(Y2+0.05), where X is the column containing the number of times a stock price has multiplied from its 52-week low (Mult) and Y is the column containing the %Lag values. You can see that this variable systematically diminishes the role of the multiple (Mult) variable in favor of the %Lag variable and thus ranks the stocks somewhat differently from the ranking provided by the MRI.
3. The Price Movement Momentum Index (PMM)
   This is another of those indices that are highly predictive of short-term gain and are thus worthy of inclusion into the Universal Index. The derivation of this index is surprisingly simple. It is

the sum of the One-Month Momentum Index (1MM) and the Adjusted Price Movement Index (APMI). The Excel formula for computation is as follows: =X2+Y2, where X is the column containing the One-Month Momentum Index (1MM) and Y is the column containing the Adjusted Price Movement Index (APMI).

4. *Beta*

    Beta is a measure of individual stock volatility *versus* overall market volatility, where a value of 1.00 signifies that the stock and the market are equal in volatility. Values above 1.00 signify volatility that is greater than market volatility. Values below 1.00 show lower volatility than that of the overall market. Thus, when the overall market moves precipitously either in a positive or a negative direction, high volatility stocks are expected to exceed the percentage move of the overall market in the same direction. Mutual funds and hedge funds that take advantage of *beta* are sometimes referred to as *beta-smart* funds. I have experimented with including *beta* in the Cumulative Technical Ranking (CTR) statistic, but currently the jury is out concerning the best way to implement *beta* in trading models that seek to rank individual stocks. When I find an appropriate derivative of this statistic, I plan to incorporate it into the Cumulative Technical Ranking (CTR) statistic.

5. The Revised Universal Index (UI)

    As indicated in Chapter Eight, the Universal Index (UI) is a composite of all of the best known predictors of future price gain as determined by methods described earlier in this book. It follows that this index should be subject to revision as better predictors are found. In Table 8.1 we can see that the Universal Index at the time of the writing of Chapter Eight consisted of eight variables; i.e., Grand Total Ranking (GR), Percentage Lag (%Lag), One-Month Percentage Growth (1MG), Adjusted Price Movement (APM), One-Month Momentum (1MM), Residual Ranking (Res), Relative Strength (RSI), and Technical-Fundamental Discrepancy (TFD). Using the improved selection criteria described above, I have subsequently dropped three of these variables from the Universal Index and have added five new variables, making a new total of ten composite variables. The variables I have dropped for lack of predictive efficacy are as follows: Grand Total Ranking (GR), Relative Strength (RSI), and Technical-Fundamental Discrepancy (TFD). The five new variables added are as follows: the Cumulative Technical Ranking (CTR), the Momentum Ratio Index (MRI), the Price Movement Momentum Index (PMM), the Momentum Lag Ratio (MLR), and the 52-Week Multiple (Mult) variable. These variables have all been operationally defined earlier, and the procedure for incorporating them into the Universal Index has been described in Chapter Eight. Of course, these new improvements should have positive implications for the implementation of trading strategies as described in Chapters Nine and Ten.

Research Needed

There are a host of yet unanswered questions in the area of stock trading and financial engineering. It is my sincere hope that some dedicated graduate students or other finance researchers will take it upon themselves to investigate these questions and provide satisfying answers. Here is a brief list of my own personal questions and problems for which answers would be as welcome as the flowers in spring.

1. How is it that some stocks have wonderful fundamentals at the same time that their technical characteristics are dismal? It seems that you can buy and hold such stocks forever to no avail. Similarly, there are stocks with fabulous technical performance that have terrible fundamentals. How is such incongruous performance possible? Is it a mistake to buy stocks that excel on one side but disappoint on the other? Is it advantageous to prefer stocks with uniform technical/fundamental rankings as opposed to stocks with divergent technical/fundamental rankings?
2. To what extent can all of the processes described in this book be automated to reduce the onerous task of data entry? I dream of watching the stock rankings adjusting automatically in real time.

Can this be done at minimal expense? Do let me know if you can do it.
3. What are the underlying differences between stocks that multiply in value nine or ten times over the course of a single year and stocks that may double in value but then go negative over the same period? What are the key determinants of such continuing positive momentum?
4. Why is it the case that positive residuals from one-month growth predictions are on average more predictive of future growth than negative residuals? In other words, why is it that stocks which exceed growth predictions continue to exceed them? And by way of exception, why are there a few stocks with the largest negative residuals that also exceed growth predictions? To some extent it may appear that absolute distance of residuals from actual price gain, regardless of direction, can also be predictive of future price gain.
5. Why is it the case that there are entire market sectors, such as biotech stocks, for which earnings appear to be negatively related to growth? To what extent are other sectors so related to growth, and what are the determinants of these negative relationships? Can and should stocks be aggregated by sector in such a way that earnings may become more predictive of positive or negative growth?
6. How and to what extent should some areas of market activity, such as derivatives and leveraging, be regulated? And what are areas of market activity where government intervention is a net negative and should not be permitted? And related to this, should politicians and other government agents and regulators be allowed to participate in insider trading schemes and other market profiteering endeavors as they are at present? How can we better track such questionable activity?
7. Whenever we create a ranking continuum on prospective profitability, we are defining a latent trait. This process becomes complicated when the underlying latent trait is multidimensional. This implies the need for studies of construct validity to test whether the measurement construct itself is valid at all points

along the measurement continuum. It may be useful to apply a one-parameter latent trait model to analyze market data and identify stocks and sectors that need to be removed as misfits to the model. A unidimensional model such as the one-parameter Rasch Model (Wright & Stone, 1979) would flag stocks that belong to other dimensions and should therefore be excluded from the system. That way results may become more dependable. Latent trait models have been used to detect examinees with improbable test response patterns that identified those examinees as cheaters. Likely similar models could be employed to find stocks with improbable performance patterns that could signal fraudulent data reporting, pump-and-dump schemes, and invalid inclusion into predictive models.

8. How may stock *beta* coefficients be used most effectively in ranking stocks for buying or selling? Although I did not find a significant correlation between *beta* and one-month growth in an earlier study, as I now look at my current stock rankings it is apparent that the top five stocks in the ranking have an average *beta* of -2.31 and the bottom five stocks have an average beta of +2.12. *Beta* is a measure of individual stock volatility *versus* overall market volatility. Clearly then, high-*beta* stocks should be advantageous in market uptrends, and low-*beta* stocks should be desirable in market downtrends. In addition, because volatility is related to liquidity, the liquidity of individual stocks should also be taken into consideration. Certainly more study is warranted regarding the benefits of positive or negative *beta* values under varying market conditions.

9. Chapter Eleven has provided comparative information on four technical timing indices. Unfortunately the information presented was highly limited because it was based on the performance of a single stock. Time and space did not permit comparisons over a much larger random sample of stocks. It could become a useful research project for an enterprising graduate student to conduct such comparative research with a much larger sample of stocks and with additional timing indicators over extended periods of observation.

10. Diversification is still a topic in need of research. Now that we can rank stocks for inclusion into a portfolio, how best can we determine the optimal number of stocks to include in a portfolio? We know that too many stocks will only serve to approximate some major market index, and too few stocks will be subject to vicissitudes of individual stock reversals. One possible research study would entail devising a series of portfolios with differing numbers of stocks chosen according to rankings obtained by a variety of methods, and then comparing their performances over differing periods of time. Such a study might address at the same time questions of optimal numbers of stocks and questions of optimal holding times, and these matters could also be related to the amount of investment capital available.

11. The mathematics involved is daunting, but I suspect that the same data assimilation techniques and nonlinear dynamic systems used in weather forecasting can profitably be applied to modeling and predicting of equities and commodities markets. Certainly some of the same challenges are present in forecasting weather and in forecasting market behavior. Someone has suggested that this problem may already have been solved surreptitiously by some creative researcher, but that the innovator is not about to share this profitable information with the public (Reich and Cotter, 2015). In any event, it would be useful for someone more qualified to spell out such applications for financial modeling.

Perspective

Backing off from this project to pause for a deep breath brings me to a few concluding thoughts. First of all, I trust this meager effort demonstrates conclusively that the stock market does not behave entirely as a random walk. There are many observable and predictable patterns of equity performance that can be and have been documented. Stocks can indeed be ranked according to the likelihood of future investment success. However, it needs to be acknowledged that equities predictions, like weather predictions, may not hold for a long time into the future.

Also, if we do not have timely input of accurate and appropriate data, our results will not always give us the answers we seek.

Finally, from the beginning of this book I have acknowledged my Christian faith, and that in turn leads me to a few important concluding thoughts. This is a book about material gain. Material gain is highly important, but it seems to me that many traders fail to realize that material gain is not the most important human pursuit. Jesus put it another way. "A man's life does not consist in the abundance of things that he possesses." And again, "What value is it if a man should gain the whole world and lose his own soul, or what can he give in exchange for his soul?" Therefore, despite the subliminal messages of our culture, always remember that "net worth" is not the same thing as "self worth." That way there can be hope that one's ego not become too inflated with success nor too deflated with failure. It is important also to diversify your holdings beyond the material realm by laying up real lasting spiritual treasure. That way too you will find that there is no need to jump off some tall building whenever there is a major market reversal.

Just as there are predictable and mathematically dependable relationships in the material realm, so too there are such relationships in the spiritual realm. I leave you with this beautiful and mathematically symmetrical Biblical formula found in James 4:8, "Draw near to God, and He will draw near to you."

My sincere best wishes to you in both your material and your spiritual pursuits.

INDEX A LIST OF TABLES

TABLE 1.1. Twenty Stocks Arranged in Ascending Order for Proximity to New 52-Week Highs on May 26, 2014.

TABLE 3.1. Twenty Stocks Arranged in Descending Order for Cumulative Momentum on June 7, 2014.

TABLE 4.1. Twenty Stocks Arranged in Descending Order of the Price Movement Index on June 20, 2014.

TABLE 5.1. Twenty Stocks Arranged in Descending Order of Positive Residuals in the Estimation of One-Month Growth on June 25, 2014.

TABLE 6.1. Twenty Stocks Arranged in Ascending Order of Cumulative Technical Ranking Index (CTR) on August 14, 2014.

TABLE 7.1. Five Fundamental Indices for 20 Stocks Arranged in Ascending Order of Cumulative Contrarian Fundamental Rank (CFR) on October 2, 2014.

TABLE 8.1. Twenty Stocks Arranged in Ascending Order of Global Total Ranking (GTO) of Combined Technical and Fundamental Indicators with Alternative PMI (APMI) and Technical-Fundamental Discrepancy Rankings (TFDr) as Noted on November 2, 2014.

TABLE 8.2. Twenty Stocks Arranged in Descending Order of Universal Index (UI) Ranking in a Database of 98 Stocks on November 21, 2014.

TABLE 10.1. Ten Trading Strategies Compared for Performance over One Week, Two Weeks, and Five Weeks (2/23/15 – 4/3/15).

TABLE 11.1. Signal Dates for Buy and Sell Decisions with Four Timing Indicators

INDEX B LIST OF FIGURES

FIGURE 5.1. Scattergram of Stocks Plotted in Relation to a Sample Regression Line Depicting the Relationship between One-Month Percentage Gain and PMI Score, with a Perpendicular Distance Line Inserted.

FIGURE 11.1 Finviz SharpChart Representation of INUV on May 15, 2015, with Critical Timing Indicators Depicted.

INDEX C RECOMMENDED WEBSITES

Website Information Available

American Bulls.Com Individual stock signals, buy/sell recommendations

Barchart.Com Technical analysis, stock signals, stock ratings

Bigcharts.Marketwatch.Com Interactive EPS/PE discrepancy charting

CBOE.Com Put/Call ratios, volatility indexes for market timing

Marketwatch.Com Fundamental data, valuation ratios

Clearstation.Etrade.Com Fundamental ratios, futures prices

Finance.Google.Com Basic stock information, delayed quotes

Finance.Yahool.Com Delayed Quotes, message boards, stock data, portfolio management

Finviz.Com Technical & fundamental stock data

Freestockcharts.Com Stock charts, portfolio management

Ino.Com Equity index futures, commodity futures

Moneycentral.msn.Com Basic stock information, portfolio management

Ragingbull.quote.Com Penny stock ratings, bulletin boards

Stockcharts.Com Stock charting, technical and fundamental scans

Vectorvest.Com Limited free stock analysis

INDEX D RECOMMENDED READINGS

Ahamed, L. *Lords of Finance: The Bankers Who Broke the World.* New York: Penguin Group, 2009.

Antonacci, G. *Dual Momentum Investing: An Innovative Strategy for Higher Returns with Lower Risk.* New York: McGraw-Hill, 2014.

Berenstein, P.L. *Against the Gods: The Remarkable Story of Risk.* New York: John Wiley & Sons, 1996.

Binnewies, R. *The Options Course: A Winning Program for Investors and Traders.* New York: Irwin Professional Publishing, 1995.

Carr, T.K. *Market-Neutral Trading: Combining Technical and Fundamental Analysis into 7 Long-Short Trading Systems.* New York: McGraw-Hill, 2014.

Elder, A. *Trading for a Living: Psychology, Trading Tactics, Money Management.* New York: Wiley & Sons, 1993.

Ferguson, N. *The Ascent of Money: A Financial History of the World.* New York: Penguin Group, 2008.

Frost, A.J. & Prechter, R.R. *Elliott Wave Principle.* Gainsville, GA: New Classics Library, 1990.

Fullman, S.H. *Options: A Personal Seminar.* New York: New York Institute of Finance/Simon & Schuster, 1992.

Graham, B. *The Intelligent Investor: A Book of Practical Counsel.* New York: Harper Collins, 2003.

Grimes, A. *The Art and Science of Technical Analysis.* Hoboken, NJ: John Wiley & Sons, 2012.

Harnet, D.L. and J.F. Horrell. *Data, Statistics, and Decision Models with Excel.* New York: John Wiley & Sons, 1998.

Henning, G. *The Value and Momentum Trader: Dynamic Stock Selection Models to Beat the Market.* Hoboken, NJ: John Wiley & Sons, 2010.

Jurik, M. ed. *Computerized Trading: Maximizing Day Trading and Overnight Profits.* New York: New York Institute of Finance, 1999.

LeFevre, E. *Reminiscences of a Stock Operator.* New York: John Wiley & Sons, 1994.

Lynch, P. *One Up on Wall Street: How to Use What You Already Know to Make Money in the Market.* New York: Penguin Books, 1989.

Markman, J.D. *Swing Trading: Power Strategies to Cut Risk and Boost Profits.* Hoboken, NJ: John Wiley & Sons, 2003.

Matrus, K. *Finding #1 Stocks: Screening, Backtesting and Time-Proven Strategies (The Zacks Series).* Hoboken, NJ: John Wiley & Sons, 2011.

Maturi, R.J. *Divining the Dow: 100 of the World's Most Widely Followed Prediction Systems.* Chicago: Probus Publishing Company, 1993.

Maturi, R.J. *Stock Picking: The 11 Best Tactics for Beating the Market.* New York: McGraw-Hill, 1993.

McAllen, F. *Charting and Technical Analysis.* Charleston, SC: Amazon Digital Services, 2012.

Murphy, J.J. *Technical Analysis of the Financial Markets: A Comprehensive Guide to Trading Methods and Applications.* New York: Prentice-Hall Press, 1999.

Nassar, D.S. *Rules of the Trade: Indispensable Insights for Online Trading.* New York: McGraw-Hill, 2001.

O'Neil, W.J. *How to Make Money in Stocks: A Winning System in Good Times or Bad.* New York: McGraw-Hill, 1995.

Peters, E.E. *Chaos and Order in the Capital Markets: A New View of Cycles, Prices, and Market Volatility.* New York: John Wiley & Sons, 1991.

Reich, S. and C. Cotter. *Probabilistic Forecasting and Bayesian Data Assimilation.* Cambridge: Cambridge University Press, 2015.

Schwager, J.D. *Market Wizards: Interviews with Top Traders.* New York: Harper & Row, 1990.

Schwager, J.D. *The New Market Wizards: Conversations with America's Top Traders.* New York: Harper Collins, 1992.

Schwager, J.D. *Stock Market Wizards: Revised and Updated.* Harper Collins, 2003.

Smith, G. *How I Trade for a Living.* New York: John Wiley & Sons, 2000.

Sperandeo, V. *Trader Vic: Methods of a Wall Street Master.* New York: John Wiley & Sons, 1993.

Sperandeo, V. *Trader Vic II: Principles of Professional Speculation.* New York: John Wiley & Sons, 1994.

Stein, B. and P. DeMuth. *Yes, You Can Time the Market.* New York: John Wiley & Sons, 2004.

Tanous, P.J. *Investment Gurus: A Road Map to Wealth from the World's Best Money Managers.* New York: New York Institute of Finance, 1997.

Train, J. *The Money Masters: Nine Great Investors: Their Winning Strategies and How You Can Apply Them.* New York: Harper & Row, 1980.

Wilder, W. *New Concepts in Technical Trading Systems.* Trend Research, 1978.

Wright, B.D. and M.H. Stone. *Best Test Design: Rasch Measurement.* Chicago: MESA Press, 1979.

Zacks, L. *The Handbook of Equity Market Anomalies: Translating Market Inefficiencies into Effective Investment Strategies.* Hoboken, NJ: John Wiley & Sons, 2011.

Zweig, M. *Winning on Wall Street: How to Spot Market Trends Early, Which Stocks to Pick, When to Buy and Sell for Peak Profits and Minimum Risk.* New York: Warner Books, Inc., 1990.

TABLE 1.1. Twenty Stocks Arranged in Ascending Order for Proximity to New 52-Week Highs on May 26, 2014.

	A	B	C	D	E	F
	Symbol	Price	High	Low	Mult	%Lag
	PAH	25.37	25.38	11.75	2.16	4E04
	THRM	42.9	42.92	16.52	2.6	5E04
	PCYG	11.97	11.98	5.05	2.37	8E04
	FUR	15.05	15.09	10.77	1.4	0.003
	ITMN	39.98	40.13	9.27	4.31	0.004
	AMKR	9.53	9.57	3.91	2.44	0.004
	PPC	25.1	25.25	11.41	2.2	0.006
	ARX	10.53	10.6	6.04	1.74	0.007
	GBX	55.5	55.87	21.1	2.63	0.007
	DAVE	31.76	31.99	11.7	2.71	0.007
	SKX	42.45	43.04	19.99	2.12	0.014
	CXDC	10.06	10.2	3.99	2.52	0.014
	WFT	21.2	21.5	12.99	1.63	0.014
	ECOL	49.65	50.37	26.68	1.86	0.014
	TSYS	3.38	3.43	2.08	1.63	0.015
	IBN	51.46	52.28	24.94	2.06	0.016
	SLCA	49.44	50.26	19.26	2.57	0.016
	MACK	7.52	7.65	2.05	3.67	0.017
	DDS	109.77	111.74	75.6	1.45	0.018
	SWC	17.46	17.78	9.78	1.79	0.018

TABLE 3.1. Twenty Stocks Arranged in Descending Order for Cumulative Momentum (CMI) on June 7, 2014

A	G	H	I	J	K	L	M	N
Symbol	1MoPr	3MoPr	1MoGn	3MoGn	ToGn	1MM	12MM	CMI
GMK	37.59	33.08	18.542	34.704	53.246	18.318	746.4	764.72
PAM	7.67	4.8	22.816	96.25	119.07	20.698	108.81	129.51
PL	51.24	52.49	35.558	32.33	67.888	34.264	70.349	104.61
HSH	35.3	37.52	66.912	57.036	123.95	57.664	10.179	67.842
MMI	15.73	17.49	42.975	28.588	71.563	40.314	26.989	67.303
CXDC	6.83	5.09	78.624	139.69	218.31	56.188	9.1712	65.359
ITMN	30.83	13.77	33.441	198.77	232.21	24.767	39.358	64.124
SSLT	11.91	11.82	74.307	75.635	149.94	46.217	5.7363	51.954
DAVE	26.79	25.58	28.331	34.402	62.733	21.399	26.527	47.926
SKX	41.12	34.63	15.175	36.76	51.935	11.598	34.178	45.776
ENG	2.1	1.58	82.857	143.04	225.9	33.352	8.9051	42.257
IDCC	34.26	31.5	37.069	49.079	86.149	28.624	9.3412	37.965
PES	14.97	11.52	9.5524	42.361	51.914	4.6981	31.697	36.395
NFX	31.83	28.19	17.122	32.245	49.368	13.381	18.257	31.638
BBW	11.93	8.25	27.913	84.97	112.88	16.895	13.855	30.75
SAIA	38.1	34.23	19.318	32.807	52.125	15.155	15.547	30.703
PHX	43.15	38.28	34.739	51.881	86.62	21.501	8.5511	30.052
SNDK	86.26	75.45	15.94	32.551	48.492	11.164	18.502	29.666
DYN	28.45	23.03	22.882	51.802	74.684	14.655	11.309	25.965
ENSG	22.12	23.03	38.969	33.478	72.447	20.137	3.3038	23.441

TABLE 4.1. Twenty Stocks Arranged in Descending Order on the Price Movement Index (PMI) on June 20, 2014.

A	B	E	F	G	H	I	J	O	P
Symbol	Price	Mult	%Lag	1MoPr	3MoPr	1MoGn	3MoGn	Num	PMI
NZ	5.41	2.76	0.022	3.63	4.25	49.036	27.294	4.6815	41.4
SYNA	91.35	2.61	5E04	57.74	61.48	58.209	48.585	5.5116	33
VNCE	37.65	1.67	0.009	24.62	26.63	52.924	41.382	4.0592	25.68
SN	38	1.86	5E04	27.69	28.1	37.234	35.231	4.6559	24.59
RH	90.2	1.65	0.002	62.84	64.78	43.539	39.241	4.3119	23.85
WLB	36.66	3.4	0.012	27.75	26.64	32.108	37.613	5.6561	23.79
AMOT	16.22	2.44	0.016	12.2	12.24	32.951	32.516	4.6294	22.98
CSCD	13.63	2.1	0.012	9.91	10.01	37.538	36.164	4.4212	22.58
BDSI	12.4	3.21	0.032	8.96	8.88	38.393	39.64	4.6561	21.59
GRH	1.81	2.41	0.032	0.97	1.02	86.598	77.451	4.0333	21.59
REX	79.38	2.97	0.019	57.38	55.08	38.341	44.118	4.9828	21.09
BLUE	40.71	2.39	0.025	27.21	26.83	49.614	51.733	4.2447	19.61
CRZO	68.25	2.54	0.004	56.11	52.23	21.636	30.672	5.2592	18.43
RMBS	14.69	1.85	0.001	11.32	10.61	29.77	38.454	4.599	17.76
LNG	68.54	2.74	0.012	57.4	53.68	19.408	27.683	5.0501	17.33
CODE	21.41	2.21	0.034	17.91	17.72	19.542	20.824	3.8065	16.85
AXDX	29.33	4.28	0.006	22.71	18.1	29.15	62.044	6.7045	15.58
GLNG	56.49	1.85	0.023	43.59	40.85	29.594	38.286	3.8041	14.02
FANG	89.79	2.92	0.038	71.15	65.68	26.198	36.708	4.2478	14.02
TWTC	40.83	1.58	0.02	32.73	31.16	24.748	31.033	3.5882	13.7

Figure 5.1. Scattergram of Stocks Plotted in Relation to a Sample Regression Line Depicting the Relationship between One-Month Percentage Gain and PMI Score, with a Perpendicular Distance Line Inserted.

TABLE 5.1. Twenty Stocks Arranged in Descending Order of Positive Residuals in the Estimation of One-Month Growth on June 25, 2014.

A	B	C	D	E	F	G	I	P	Q	R
Symbol	Price	High	Low	Mult	%Lag	1MoPr	1MoGn	PMI	E1MGn	Resid
SYPR	5.86	6.5	2.52	2.33	0.098	2.95	98.644	9.02	26.7	71.94
GRH	1.88	2.03	0.75	2.51	0.074	0.99	89.899	12.12	23.04	66.86
BLUE	39.41	41.75	17.03	2.31	0.056	23.35	68.779	13.33	21.61	47.17
OMER	17.53	18.01	4.75	3.69	0.027	11.55	51.775	23.87	9.173	42.6
RH	92.37	93.54	54.61	1.69	0.013	66.08	39.785	27.38	5.034	34.75
GWPH	96.14	97.64	8.5	11.3	0.015	68.76	39.82	27.12	5.337	34.48
GLOG	31.65	32.44	12.56	2.52	0.024	23.14	36.776	22.03	11.35	25.43
LOAN	3.31	3.33	1.42	2.33	0.006	2.36	40.254	14.43	20.31	19.94
TAT	11.08	11.53	6.7	1.65	0.039	8.21	34.957	17.76	16.39	18.57
MMI	25.75	26.64	13.09	1.97	0.033	18.41	39.87	12.94	22.08	17.79
MMYT	34.25	34.91	13.02	2.63	0.019	25.94	32.035	19.27	14.6	17.43
SSLT	19.14	21.36	7.95	2.41	0.104	12.98	47.458	6.021	30.24	17.21
MARK	8.7	9.11	2.24	3.88	0.045	6.27	38.756	12.87	22.16	16.59
FOLD	3.03	3.1	1.77	1.71	0.023	2.21	37.104	13.32	21.63	15.47
BFR	11.8	12.08	3.61	3.27	0.023	8.9	32.584	17.12	17.14	15.44
MVG	9.46	10.64	4.87	1.94	0.111	6.96	35.92	12.05	23.13	12.79
VNCE	35.54	38	22.53	1.58	0.065	25.88	37.326	9.176	26.52	10.81
EDAP	4.44	4.52	2.38	1.87	0.018	3.31	34.139	11.64	23.6	10.54
IDCC	47.31	49.1	26.25	1.8	0.036	35.3	34.023	10.36	25.12	8.906
SYNA	89.38	91.5	37.87	2.36	0.023	67.78	31.868	12.03	23.15	8.715

TABLE 6.1. Twenty Stocks Arranged in Ascending Order of Cumulative Technical Ranking Index (CTR) on August 14, 2014.

Symbol	PMI	CMI	RSI	PMIr	CMIr	RSIr	CTI	CTR
PBYI	54.65	1015.84	83.04	1	1	8	10	1
RIC	17.44	223.16	83.69	14	15	7	36	2
BITA	13.03	548.33	88.56	31	5	1	37	3
ZEN	18.56	141.18	84.38	9	27	5	41	4
PLNR	18.44	191.10	79.00	10	19	16	45	5
PCRX	17.98	214.34	79.13	13	17	15	45	5
SLI	39.31	126.02	80.24	7	33	10	50	6
X	16.24	125.42	86.45	17	34	3	54	7
TSRA	20.29	86.78	84.29	5	50	6	61	8
HTCH	20.00	152.73	75.11	6	25	32	63	9
XRS	14.30	216.66	76.85	24	16	23	63	9
SPCB	23.65	226.55	71.18	2	14	50	66	10
CQB	18.38	68.03	86.62	11	57	2	70	11
PTRY	14.09	122.51	80.08	27	35	11	73	12
NVEC	17.19	50.06	77.29	15	67	22	104	13
FDO	15.27	68.44	74.35	19	56	34	109	14
SKX	14.21	131.47	70.75	26	31	53	110	15
TWOU	15.62	80.33	68.88	18	52	61	131	16
PTCT	7.45	154.73	68.81	54	24	62	140	17
SNSS	11.83	100.62	65.25	33	43	75	151	18

TABLE 7.1. Five Fundamental Indices for 20 Stocks Arranged in Ascending Order of Cumulative Contrarian Fundamental Rank (CFR) on October 2, 2014.

A	Y	Z	AA	AB	AC	AD	AE	AF	AG	AH	AI	AJ
Symbol	PSR	EPS	5YSG	ROA	PM	PSRr	EPSr	5YSr	ROAr	PMr	CmFr	CFR
FOLD	430.48	-0.98	-51.6	-53.7	0	2	13	1	5	21	42	1
RCPT	361.73	-3.72	0	-61.1	0	3	2	16	3	21	45	2
TTPH	66.37	-2.21	0	-60.9	0	5	4	16	4	21	50	3
PIP	8.76	-0.21	-11.5	-65.4	-75.9	17	28	8	2	1	56	4
AGIO	76.9	-2.06	0	-28.3	0	4	6	16	14	21	61	5
RDUS	5	-29.84	0	-289.8	0	22	1	16	1	21	61	5
EXAS	751.99	-0.79	0	-35	0	1	14	16	12	21	64	7
TRUE	10.78	-0.53	0	-20.1	-21.6	15	19	16	16	4	70	8
OVAS	5	-1.87	0	-51.4	0	22	8	16	6	21	73	9
ESPR	5	-2.08	0	-42	0	22	5	16	9	21	73	9
BBLU	24.07	-0.58	0	-38.4	0	10	17	16	10	21	74	11
FLXN	5	-1.42	0	-43.5	0	22	12	16	8	21	79	12
MSON	5.06	-0.26	-18.5	-8.4	-9.2	21	26	4	22	7	80	13
MNDL	8.87	-0.54	4	-49.8	-70.7	16	18	37	7	2	80	13
IDSY	2.03	-0.64	-10.6	-13.8	-17.6	36	15	9	20	6	86	15
ZLTQ	6.41	-0.35	0	-14.9	-8.9	19	25	16	19	9	88	16
VRTX	30.05	-2.03	47.2	-20.5	-56.9	9	7	57	15	3	91	17
HTCH	0.47	-1.79	-16.9	-17.3	-19.6	56	9	6	17	5	93	18
RAIL	1.19	-1.55	-17.2	-4.8	-5.3	42	11	5	28	12	98	19
PTCT	32.28	-2.35	112.5	-30.3	0	8	3	59	13	21	104	20

TABLE 8.1. Twenty Stocks Arranged in Ascending Order of Global Total Ranking (GTO) of Combined Technical and Fundamental Indicators with Alternative PMI (APMI) and Technical-Fundamental Discrepancy Rankings (TFDr) As Noted on November 2, 2014.

A	B	X	AJ	AK	AL	AM	AN	AO
Symbol	Price	CTR	CFR	T+F	GTO	APMI	TFD	TFDr
RCPT	101.1	1	11	12	1	46.14	11	4
AGIO	83.75	3	14	17	2	52.38	13	5
RENT	80.45	13	6	19	3	22.23	10	2
ANAC	30.01	7	13	20	4	23.12	10	2
INFN	14.61	4	26	30	5	22.27	27	11
ESPR	29.34	15	16	31	6	26.56	7	1
IMDZ	29.55	29	4	33	7	4.66	32	13
MSON	13.85	32	2	34	8	6.71	38	15
RGLS	18.19	23	11	34	8	1.27	20	7
IG	9.93	16	22	38	10	42.64	16	6
STRP	20	38	5	43	11	6.71	44	20
VASC	29.39	9	36	45	12	25.44	39	16
TTPH	25.02	35	10	45	12	9.72	37	14
MACK	9.49	19	29	48	14	40.15	24	9
BBW	17.15	10	38	48	14	21.08	42	18
TRNX	27.94	18	31	49	16	13.93	29	12
ZLTQ	25.27	41	8	49	16	6	49	23
PTRY	26.09	12	39	51	18	20.47	45	22
LEAF	37.1	23	28	51	18	13.76	23	8
OVAS	20.49	5	49	54	20	29.03	64	34

TABLE 8.2. Twenty Stocks Arranged in Descending Order of Universal Index (UI) Ranking in a Database of 98 Stocks on November 21, 2014.

A	R	AP	AQ	AR	AS	AT	AU	AV	AW	AX	AY	AZ	BA
Symb	Res	Rr	MG	1MM	GR	%Lag	1MG	APM	1MM	Res	RSI	TFD	UI
RDCM	40.24	95	2	2	1	1	1	1	1	1	-1	1	1	6
PAYC	20.16	85	4	4	1	1	1	1	1	1	-1	1	1	6
MRGE	-12.4	3	16	6	1	1	0	1	1	1	1	-1	0	4
AMOT	-5.73	17	13	5	0	1	1	1	1	1	0	1	-1	4
ODP	-3.85	23	33	10	1	1	0	1	1	1	0	-1	1	4
INCY	0.31	40	22	7	1	1	0	0	1	1	0	0	1	4
RDI	-4.84	20	37	14	0	1	0	0	1	1	0	1	0	3
RCPT	43.47	96	3	3	1	0	1	1	1	1	-1	-1	1	3
CTP	-3.67	25	12	11	1	0	1	1	1	1	0	-1	0	3
RIC	-8.89	10	54	42	1	0	-1	1	-1	1	1	0	1	2
ANIP	45.98	97	1	1	0	0	1	1	1	1	-1	1	-1	2
OVAS	26.96	92	7	13	1	-1	1	1	1	1	-1	0	0	2
YHOO	-1.86	30	38	19	0	1	0	0	0	0	0	1	0	2
ABMD	6.87	62	15	8	0	0	0	0	1	1	-1	1	0	1
AGIO	15.3	77	20	35	1	0	0	1	0	0	-1	-1	1	1
NXTM	-7.57	12	69	52	0	0	-1	0	-1	-1	1	1	1	1
ZLTQ	-3.18	26	61	36	1	0	-1	0	0	0	0	-1	1	0
SWIR	9.08	67	18	27	1	-1	0	-1	0	-1	1	1	0
MIK	0.76	42	53	17	0	1	-1	0	0	-1	1	-1	-1
KONA	7.93	64	21	16	0	0	0	-1	0	-1	0	1	-1

TABLE 10.1. Ten Trading Strategies Compared for Performance over One Week, Two Weeks, and Five Weeks (2/28/15-4/3/15)

Trading Strategy	Percentage Gain (Loss)		
Momentum Strategies	One Week	Two Weeks	Five Weeks
1. The Percentage Lag Strategy	4.84	7.88	0.26
2. The One-Month Momentum Strategy	0.32	2.35	11.72
3. The Cumulative Momentum Strategy	0.37	3.78	10.76
4. The Multiple-Ratio Momentum Strategy	(-2.15)	1.90	5.14
5. The Patterned Price Movement Strategy	(-1.06)	1.55	10.70
Performance Strategies			
6. The One-Month Gain Strategy	0.44	3.19	11.01
7. The Universal Index Strategy	1.20	2.68	12.12
8. The Global Total Performance Strategy	(-1.16)	1.12	6.45
9. The Comprehensive Performance Strategy	(-0.44)	2.34	6.50
10. The Future Trend Strategy	1.26	2.17	14.37
Major Indices			
11. The S&P 500 Index	(-1.56)	(-2.49)	(-1.64)
12. The Dow Jones Industrial Average	(-1.52)	(-2.16)	(-2.04)

Figure 11.1. Finviz SharpChart Representation of INUV on May 15, 2015, with Critical Timing Indicators Depicted (Courtesy of StockCharts.com). (Note, be sure to log in to the website in case the colors are not reproduced in this printing.)

TABLE 11.1. Signal Dates for Buy and Sell Decisions with Four Timing Indicators

Indicator	Buy	Sell
RSI	1/25, 2/3*, 2/26*, 5/12*	4/1, 4/16
Volume	2/4*, 3/2, 3/28, 4/4*, 5/13*	4/1, 4/12*, 4/19, 5/17
MACD	1/24*, 3/1, 4/27, 5/11*, 5/13*	2/23, 4/13*, 4/18
ADX	1/29, 2/28*, 4/29	2/25, 4/23

*Indicates profitable signals.

Made in United States
North Haven, CT
30 April 2025